Easier Exam in Arithmetic

CROSS GREEN SCHOOL
CROSS GREEN LANE
LEEDS LS9 0BB

The following titles by Ewart Smith are also available from the same publishers:

Examples in Arithmetic

A New General Arithmetic
    Part A
    Part B
    Answers
    Complete Volume

Examples in Mathematics
    Book 1
    Book 2

Easier Examples in Arithmetic

Ewart Smith MSc
Head of Mathematics Department
Tredegar Comprehensive School

Stanley Thornes (Publishers) Ltd

© Ewart Smith 1985

All rights reserved. No part of this publication may be reproduced, stored in a retrieval system or transmitted in any form or by any means, electronic, mechanical, photocopying, recording or otherwise, without the prior written consent of the copyright holders. Applications for such permission should be addressed to the publishers: Stanley Thornes (Publishers) Ltd, Old Station Drive, Leckhampton Road, CHELTENHAM GL53 0DN.

First published 1985 by:
Stanley Thornes (Publishers) Ltd
Old Station Drive
Leckhampton
CHELTENHAM GL53 0DN

A separate Answers Booklet is available from the Publishers on request.

British Library Cataloguing in Publication Data

Smith, Ewart
   Easier examples in arithmetic.
   1. Arithmetic — Examinations, questions, etc.
   I. Title
513'.076   QA139

ISBN 0-85950-184-1

Typeset by Tech-Set, Gateshead, Tyne and Wear.
Printed and bound in Great Britain at The Bath Press, Avon.

CONTENTS

Part 1: Exercises

		Page
1.	Whole Numbers	1
2.	Place Value	3
3.	Darts and Snooker	5
4.	Fractions I	10
5.	Fractions II	13
6.	Fractions III	15
7.	Further Fractions	17
8.	Decimals	19
9.	Fractions and Decimals	23
10.	Negative Numbers	24
11.	Approximations, Decimal Places, Standard Form, Significant Figures	26
12.	Money	30
13.	Money — The Four Rules	33
14.	Shopping	38
15.	Metric Quantities	41
16.	Percentages	45
17.	Buying and Selling	48
18.	Ratio and Proportion	51
19.	Averages	54
20.	Distance, Time and Speed	56
21.	Travel Graphs	63
22.	Area by Counting Squares	66
23.	Perimeter and Area by Calculation	70
24.	Volume and Capacity	77
25.	Imperial Units	82
26.	Metric and Imperial Conversions	85
27.	Value Added Tax (VAT)	92
28.	Bills	94
29.	Insurance	98
30.	Wages and Salaries	101
31.	Budgeting, or 'Where the Money Goes'	105
32.	Banks and Building Societies	107
33.	Rental Charges	111
34.	Hire Purchase and Mortgages	113
35.	Rates and Rateable Value	117
36.	Cost of Running a Motorcycle or Car	121
37.	Life Assurance	123
38.	Simple and Compound Interest	125
39.	The Calendar, Time and Time Zones	127

40. Bus and Train Timetables — 134
41. Package Holidays — 136
42. Foreign Currency — 139
43. Appreciation and Depreciation (Increase and Decrease in Value) — 142
44. Statistics — 144

Part 2: Revision Papers 1–20

Revision Paper 1 — 154
Revision Paper 2 — 155
Revision Paper 3 — 156
Revision Paper 4 — 157
Revision Paper 5 — 158
Revision Paper 6 — 159
Revision Paper 7 — 160
Revision Paper 8 — 161
Revision Paper 9 — 162
Revision Paper 10 — 163
Revision Paper 11 — 164
Revision Paper 12 — 165
Revision Paper 13 — 166
Revision Paper 14 — 167
Revision Paper 15 — 168
Revision Paper 16 — 169
Revision Paper 17 — 170
Revision Paper 18 — 171
Revision Paper 19 — 172
Revision Paper 20 — 173

PREFACE

The success of *Examples in Arithmetic*, together with suggestions from several teachers, has led me to believe that there is a need for a similar book containing easier examples but which is not aimed at any particular external examination. *Easier Examples in Arithmetic* is an attempt to satisfy this need.

In recent years the electronic calculator has come into its own and is the potential friend of every citizen. While it is hoped that many of the exercises in this book will be worked without using a calculating aid, it should be accepted that its use will remove the drudgery from calculations for many who find real difficulty in manipulating numbers. The calculator will perform the calculations accurately leaving the operator able to concentrate his or her efforts on problem solving.

Many of the illustrations, drawings and tables can be used as a source of additional questions of the types given in the accompanying exercises.

My thanks are due to my former colleague Mr Tom Thomas for checking the answers and making several useful suggestions.

Ewart Smith
1985

Part 1 EXERCISES

1 WHOLE NUMBERS

Write the following numbers in figures:

1. Fifteen
2. Twenty-four
3. Thirty-seven
4. Forty-one
5. Fifty-three
6. Eighty-eight
7. Seventy-five
8. Ninety
9. Twenty-seven
10. Thirty-six
11. One hundred and twenty
12. Three hundred and fifty
13. Four hundred and eighty
14. Two hundred and thirty-two
15. Five hundred and seventy-six
16. Seven hundred and eighteen
17. Two hundred and seven
18. Three hundred and sixty-three
19. Two thousand, three hundred and eighteen
20. One thousand and eighty-six

Write the following numbers in words:

21. 17
22. 28
23. 32
24. 45
25. 56
26. 82
27. 77
28. 64
29. 50
30. 93
31. 160
32. 240
33. 390
34. 125
35. 243
36. 574
37. 404
38. 1400
39. 2360
40. 5178

A telephonist was given the following numbers. Write them in figures:

41. two two four four nine four
42. eight two seven six five four
43. double six, double six, four five
44. treble eight, four four two
45. seven two six, double three, seven six five

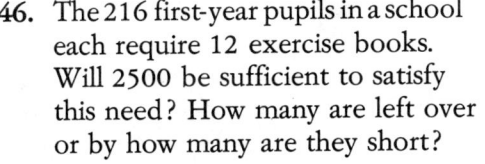

46. The 216 first-year pupils in a school each require 12 exercise books. Will 2500 be sufficient to satisfy this need? How many are left over or by how many are they short?

47. A doctor gives a patient a bottle containing 100 tablets with instructions to take two each morning and evening. How many days will the tablets last?

48. In the washroom of a hotel they estimate that 35 paper towels are used each hour between 7.00 pm and 11.00 pm. How many complete evenings will a box of 1000 last?

49. At the general election 24 500 voted for Kenwood, 12 345 for Spartan and 8246 for Whitehead. If 45 720 were entitled to vote, how many failed to do so?

50. Twenty-three people are on a coach when it leaves the bus station. 12 get on at the first stage while 7 get off; 15 get on and 6 get off at the second stage. At the third stage 2 get off but only 17 are allowed on since standing passengers are not permitted. At the fourth stage 21 get off and 8 get on. The next stop is the terminus.

How many passengers will the bus seat?
How many passengers get off at the terminus?

2 PLACE VALUE

Write down the value of the first figure in each of the following numbers:

1. In the number 437 the 4 has a value of 400.

2. 46
3. 93
4. 81
5. 55
6. 743
7. 627
8. 824
9. 555
10. 139

Write down the value of the second figure in each of the following numbers:

11. In the number 437 the 3 has a value of 30.
12. 96
13. 54
14. 347
15. 892
16. 675
17. 943
18. 2640
19. 8261
20. 5430
21. 1760
22. 5280
23. 44 000
24. 83 500
25. 76 593

Write down the value of the figure which is underlined in each of the following numbers:

26. 6_8_
27. _7_3
28. 1_4_2
29. _3_64
30. _5_370
31. _4_794
32. 63_9_8
33. 22_4_37
34. 1_5_ 000
35. 42 7_3_4

36. Add 10 to each of these numbers:
    44,   163,   249,   1730,   7364,   2395
37. Add 100 to each of these numbers:
    746,   854,   2246,   18 495,   6200,   4963
38. Take away 10 from each of these numbers:
    64,   173,   246,   3392,   4728,   1507
39. Take away 100 from each of these numbers:
    524,   2437,   8290,   1714,   29 473,   6076
40. Add 1000 to each of these numbers:
    5542,   8264,   13 474,   53 216,   88 000,   19 824
41. Take away 1000 from each of these numbers:
    2374,   7349,   15 600,   42 743,   58 000,   30 670

3

Find the following:

42. 4000 + 34 = 4034
43. 7000 + 106 = 7106

44. 700 + 3
45. 900 + 4
46. 500 + 11

47. 3000 + 27
48. 6000 + 50
49. 8000 + 400

50. 5000 + 370
51. 8000 + 104
52. 4000 + 36

53. 9000 + 174
54. 2000 + 8
55. 20 000 + 540

Complete the following statements:

56. In the number 7043 there are no hundreds.
57. In the number 50 204 there are no tens and there are no ten thousands.
58. In the number 1054 there are no...
59. In the number 706 there are no...
60. In the number 840 there are no...
61. In the number 2200 there are no...
62. In the number 3094 there are no...
63. In the number 50 472 there are no...
64. In the number 3070 there are no...
65. In the number 66 000 there are no...

3 DARTS AND SNOOKER

A. DARTS

Find the value of:

1. the double to the right of the 20
2. the treble to the right of the 7
3. the double below the 14
4. the double above the 13
5. the treble below the 10
6. the treble above the 9
7. What is the maximum possible score with three darts?
8. What is the minimum score possible with three darts if each dart scores?
9. What is the maximum possible score with three darts if each score is different?
10. What is the maximum score with two darts in adjacent areas?
11. What is the maximum score with two darts excluding doubles and trebles?
12. What is the total score of all the numbers in the first quadrant?

13. What is the total score of all the numbers in the second quadrant?

14. What is the total score of all the numbers in the third quadrant?

15. What is the total score of all the numbers in the fourth quadrant?

16. What is the total score of all the numbers on the board?

17. What is the highest score possible from two numbers next to each other (not counting doubles and trebles)? Which pair(s) of numbers give you this score?

18. What is the lowest score possible from two numbers next to each other (excluding doubles and trebles)? Which pair(s) of numbers give you this score?

19. Joe and Barry play darts, each requiring 301 to win. Their scores are:

	Joe	Barry
First throw	53	84
Second throw	76	42
Third throw	83	14
Fourth throw	6	73

(a) Who is leading after three throws, and by how much?

(b) How many does Joe require to go out with his fifth throw?

(c) How could Barry go out on his fifth throw if he must finish on a double?

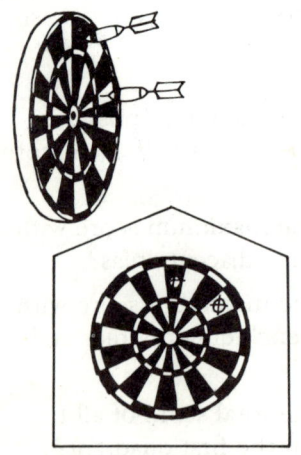

6

20. Rita and Angela play darts, each requiring 301 to win. Their scores are:

	Rita	Angela
First throw	47	66
Second throw	56	38
Third throw	14	54
Fourth throw	88	36

(a) Who is leading after three throws, and by how much?
(b) How many does Angela need to go out after her fourth throw? Can she do so with three darts?

21. Paul and Peter wish to score 301. Their scores are given in the table:

	Peter		Paul	
First throw	double	18		12
		4		5
	treble	12		19
Second throw		16	treble	20
		14		1
	double	5		18
Third throw	treble	6		9
		20	treble	12
		18		13
Fourth throw	treble	18	double	18
		13	bull's eye	
	double	16		14

(a) Who is leading after the first throw and by how much?
(b) Who is leading after the third throw and by how much?
(c) How much does each require after his fourth throw to complete the game?
(d) What is the least number of darts Paul requires to finish if he must finish on a double?

22. Chris and Linda wish to score 301. Their scores are given below:

	Chris		Linda	
First throw		6		5
		18		9
		3	double	12
Second throw		14		19
	treble	16		14
		9	double	6

Third throw		15		16
	double	4	double	20
		18		5
Fourth throw	treble	14		16
		10		7
		3		13

(a) Who is leading after the second throw and by how much?
(b) Who is leading after the fourth throw and by how much?
(c) Could Chris reach the required total next time he throws?
(d) What would he need to go out on a double?

B. SNOOKER

The scores in a snooker competition are shown in the table. The player from each section with the most points goes through to the next round.

Round 1 — Semi-final — Final

Section 1
Knowles	47	54	93
Higgins	63	72	29
Charlton	15	80	39
Taylor	71	84	27

Semi-final: 50 92 / 73 29

Section 2
Donaldson	9	54	82
Davis	62	93	37
Meo	46	18	26
Thorburn	11	50	92

Final: 53 37 93 / 43 82 44

Section 3
Williams	43	18	95
Reardon	54	104	72
Stevens	65	15	82
Virgo	21	48	23

Semi-final: 16 93 / 81 34

Section 4
Griffiths	84	62	15
Werbenuik	37	54	87
Spencer	50	23	62
Mountjoy	114	9	54

1. Copy and complete this table and hence find the winner.
2. Who scored (a) the highest total, (b) the lowest total, in the first round?
3. Whose 'frame score' was the highest? What was it?

The points value of each 'colour' in the questions that follow is:

Red	1	Blue	5
Yellow	2	Pink	6
Green	3	Black	7
Brown	4		

4. Meo makes a break of eight reds, taking a black with seven of them and a yellow with the other. How much was the break?
5. Reardon makes a break of 12 reds, taking a black with ten of them and a blue with each of the other two. How much was the break?
6. Thorne takes three reds, each with a black, followed by all the colours. How much was the break?
7. Higgins clears the table after his partner has broken off, taking a black with each of the 15 reds. How much was his break?
8. Griffiths pots the following balls in the order given: red, black, red, black, red, green, red, pink, red, blue, yellow, green, brown and blue. What break did he make?
9. Stevens pots the following balls in the order given: red, blue, red, black, red, pink, red, black, red, black, red. What break did he make?
10. Davis takes the last five reds, each with a black, followed by all the colours. How much was the break?

4 FRACTIONS I

Make the following fractions as simple as possible:

1. $\dfrac{8}{12} = \dfrac{2}{3}$

2. $\dfrac{20}{25} = \dfrac{4}{5}$

3. $\dfrac{10}{15}$ 6. $\dfrac{12}{16}$ 9. $\dfrac{100}{75}$ 12. $\dfrac{27}{36}$

4. $\dfrac{20}{24}$ 7. $\dfrac{15}{25}$ 10. $\dfrac{20}{40}$

5. $\dfrac{6}{8}$ 8. $\dfrac{60}{50}$ 11. $\dfrac{12}{20}$

Which of the following pairs of fractions is the greater?

13. $\dfrac{1}{2}, \dfrac{1}{4}$ 16. $\dfrac{1}{8}, \dfrac{1}{9}$ 19. $\dfrac{3}{5}, \dfrac{2}{5}$ 22. $\dfrac{11}{16}, \dfrac{3}{4}$

14. $\dfrac{1}{2}, \dfrac{3}{4}$ 17. $\dfrac{1}{16}, \dfrac{1}{15}$ 20. $\dfrac{1}{3}, \dfrac{5}{12}$ 23. $\dfrac{1}{8}, \dfrac{1}{2}$

15. $\dfrac{1}{2}, \dfrac{2}{3}$ 18. $\dfrac{9}{16}, \dfrac{5}{8}$ 21. $\dfrac{3}{4}, \dfrac{13}{16}$ 24. $\dfrac{17}{20}, \dfrac{4}{5}$

Which of the following pairs of fractions is the smaller?

25. $\dfrac{1}{3}, \dfrac{1}{2}$ 27. $\dfrac{7}{12}, \dfrac{3}{4}$ 29. $\dfrac{1}{5}, \dfrac{1}{6}$ 31. $\dfrac{6}{25}, \dfrac{1}{5}$

26. $\dfrac{1}{10}, \dfrac{1}{12}$ 28. $\dfrac{7}{20}, \dfrac{1}{4}$ 30. $\dfrac{1}{2}, \dfrac{7}{16}$ 32. $\dfrac{3}{5}, \dfrac{2}{3}$

Express each of the following as an improper fraction:

33. $2\frac{1}{2} = \frac{5}{2}$

34. $3\frac{1}{3}$
35. $4\frac{1}{4}$
36. $5\frac{2}{3}$

37. $6\frac{3}{4}$
38. $7\frac{3}{5}$
39. $8\frac{7}{10}$

40. $3\frac{4}{7}$
41. $2\frac{5}{12}$
42. $3\frac{5}{8}$

43. $5\frac{7}{8}$
44. $3\frac{5}{6}$
45. $3\frac{1}{4}$

Express each of the following as mixed or whole numbers:

46. $\frac{11}{5} = 2\frac{1}{5}$

47. $\frac{24}{5}$
48. $\frac{11}{3}$
49. $\frac{15}{7}$

50. $\frac{23}{6}$
51. $\frac{19}{4}$
52. $\frac{11}{2}$

53. $\frac{21}{3}$
54. $\frac{16}{5}$
55. $\frac{28}{7}$

11

The following questions refer to a bar of chocolate 6 squares by 4 squares. The shaded part is what I keep; the unshaded part is what I give away. In each case give, in as simple a fraction as possible, (a) the fraction I keep, (b) the fraction I give away.

56.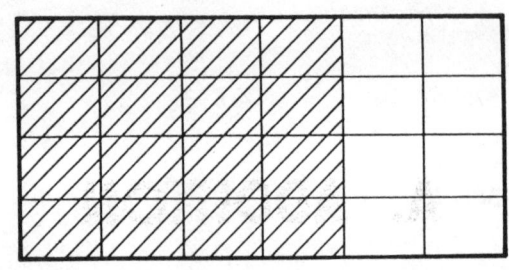

(a) $\dfrac{16}{24} = \dfrac{2}{3}$ (b) $\dfrac{8}{24} = \dfrac{1}{3}$

57.    63.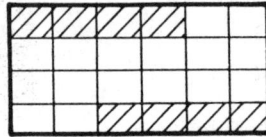

58. 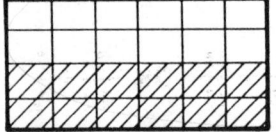   64.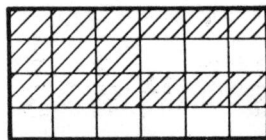

59. 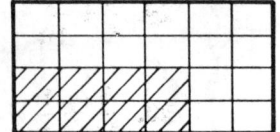   65.

60.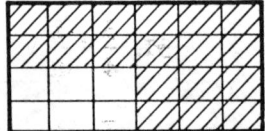

61.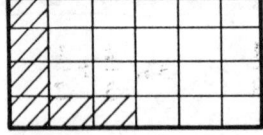

62.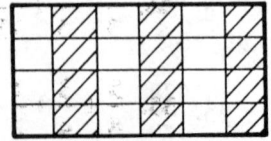

12

5 FRACTIONS II

A. ADDITION

Add the following, giving your answers in their lowest terms:

1. $\dfrac{1}{2} + \dfrac{1}{2}$

2. $\dfrac{1}{4} + \dfrac{1}{4} + \dfrac{1}{4}$

3. $\dfrac{1}{5} + \dfrac{1}{5} + \dfrac{1}{5}$

4. $\dfrac{1}{2} + \dfrac{1}{2} + \dfrac{1}{2}$

5. $\dfrac{3}{4} + \dfrac{3}{4}$

6. $\dfrac{3}{4} + \dfrac{1}{4}$

7. $\dfrac{2}{5} + \dfrac{3}{5}$

8. $\dfrac{5}{7} + \dfrac{2}{7}$

9. $\dfrac{5}{8} + \dfrac{1}{8}$

10. $\dfrac{13}{20} + \dfrac{7}{20}$

11. $\dfrac{1}{6} + \dfrac{5}{6}$

12. $\dfrac{2}{15} + \dfrac{7}{15}$

13. $\dfrac{3}{10} + \dfrac{9}{10}$

14. $\dfrac{3}{11} + \dfrac{5}{11}$

15. $\dfrac{11}{13} + \dfrac{2}{13}$

16. $\dfrac{4}{5} + \dfrac{3}{5} + \dfrac{1}{5}$

17. $\dfrac{2}{9} + \dfrac{2}{9} + \dfrac{2}{9}$

18. $\dfrac{1}{7} + \dfrac{3}{7} + \dfrac{4}{7}$

19. $\dfrac{1}{8} + \dfrac{3}{8} + \dfrac{5}{8}$

20. $\dfrac{2}{15} + \dfrac{7}{15} + \dfrac{11}{15}$

21. $\dfrac{1}{2} + \dfrac{1}{4}$

22. $\dfrac{1}{3} + \dfrac{1}{6}$

23. $\dfrac{1}{2} + \dfrac{1}{3}$

24. $\dfrac{1}{6} + \dfrac{2}{3}$

25. $\dfrac{1}{2} + \dfrac{1}{4} + \dfrac{1}{8}$

26. $\dfrac{5}{8} + \dfrac{1}{4}$

27. $\dfrac{3}{8} + \dfrac{1}{2}$

28. $\dfrac{5}{12} + \dfrac{1}{3}$

29. $\dfrac{2}{5} + \dfrac{1}{10}$

30. $\dfrac{3}{20} + \dfrac{1}{4}$

31. $\dfrac{3}{4} + \dfrac{1}{8}$

32. $\dfrac{7}{8} + \dfrac{1}{2}$

33. $\dfrac{2}{3} + \dfrac{1}{2}$

34. $\dfrac{2}{3} + \dfrac{1}{5} + \dfrac{2}{15}$

35. $\dfrac{5}{8} + \dfrac{3}{4} + \dfrac{1}{2}$

B. SUBTRACTION

Find the following, giving your answers in their lowest terms:

1. $\dfrac{3}{4} - \dfrac{1}{4}$

2. $\dfrac{3}{5} - \dfrac{2}{5}$

3. $\dfrac{2}{3} - \dfrac{1}{3}$

4. $\dfrac{4}{5} - \dfrac{1}{5}$

5. $\dfrac{4}{7} - \dfrac{3}{7}$

6. $\dfrac{5}{9} - \dfrac{2}{9}$

7. $\dfrac{7}{10} - \dfrac{1}{10}$

8. $\dfrac{11}{12} - \dfrac{7}{12}$

9. $\dfrac{9}{10} - \dfrac{3}{10}$

10. $\dfrac{7}{8} - \dfrac{3}{8}$

11. $\dfrac{7}{8} - \dfrac{1}{8}$

12. $\dfrac{7}{11} - \dfrac{5}{11}$

13. $\dfrac{11}{15} - \dfrac{1}{15}$

14. $\dfrac{7}{20} - \dfrac{3}{20}$

15. $\dfrac{19}{25} - \dfrac{7}{25}$

16. $\dfrac{31}{36} - \dfrac{19}{36}$

17. $1 - \dfrac{7}{10}$

18. $1 - \dfrac{3}{5}$

19. $1 - \dfrac{7}{20}$

20. $1 - \dfrac{3}{8}$

21. $\dfrac{1}{2} - \dfrac{1}{4}$

22. $\dfrac{1}{2} - \dfrac{1}{8}$

23. $\dfrac{1}{2} - \dfrac{1}{6}$

24. $\dfrac{1}{2} - \dfrac{1}{3}$

25. $\dfrac{1}{3} - \dfrac{1}{6}$

26. $\dfrac{2}{3} - \dfrac{1}{6}$

27. $\dfrac{5}{6} - \dfrac{2}{3}$

28. $\dfrac{3}{10} - \dfrac{1}{5}$

29. $\dfrac{2}{5} - \dfrac{3}{10}$

30. $\dfrac{5}{8} - \dfrac{1}{2}$

31. $\dfrac{7}{8} - \dfrac{3}{4}$

32. $\dfrac{7}{10} - \dfrac{2}{5}$

33. $\dfrac{7}{12} - \dfrac{1}{3}$

34. $\dfrac{7}{8} - \dfrac{1}{2}$

35. $\dfrac{2}{3} - \dfrac{3}{5}$

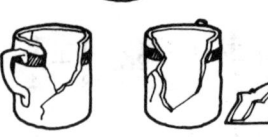

6 FRACTIONS III

A. MULTIPLICATION

Find the following, giving your answers in their lowest terms:

1. $\dfrac{1}{2} \times \dfrac{1}{4}$
2. $\dfrac{1}{2} \times \dfrac{1}{3}$
3. $\dfrac{2}{3} \times \dfrac{1}{2}$
4. $\dfrac{1}{2} \times \dfrac{3}{5}$
5. $\dfrac{2}{7} \times \dfrac{1}{3}$
6. $\dfrac{2}{3} \times \dfrac{2}{5}$
7. $\dfrac{1}{2} \times \dfrac{3}{4}$

8. $\dfrac{2}{3} \times \dfrac{3}{4}$
9. $\dfrac{5}{7} \times \dfrac{3}{5}$
10. $\dfrac{3}{8} \times \dfrac{4}{5}$
11. $\dfrac{7}{12} \times \dfrac{4}{7}$
12. $\dfrac{9}{10} \times \dfrac{2}{3}$
13. $\dfrac{5}{12} \times \dfrac{3}{5}$
14. $\dfrac{9}{11} \times \dfrac{11}{21}$

15. $\dfrac{7}{16} \times \dfrac{4}{7}$
16. $\dfrac{3}{5} \times \dfrac{10}{21}$
17. $\dfrac{12}{19} \times \dfrac{5}{12}$
18. $\dfrac{7}{24} \times \dfrac{8}{49}$
19. $\dfrac{13}{5} \times \dfrac{7}{26}$
20. $\dfrac{8}{3} \times \dfrac{3}{4}$
21. $\dfrac{2}{3} \times \dfrac{9}{5}$

22. $\dfrac{7}{15} \times \dfrac{5}{4}$
23. $\dfrac{21}{20} \times \dfrac{5}{7}$
24. $\dfrac{5}{13} \times \dfrac{8}{5}$
25. $\dfrac{7}{6} \times \dfrac{9}{14}$
26. $\dfrac{3}{8} \times \dfrac{4}{9}$
27. $\dfrac{9}{4} \times \dfrac{2}{3}$
28. $\dfrac{25}{17} \times \dfrac{34}{35}$

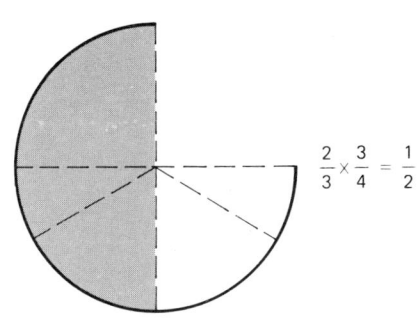

B. DIVISION

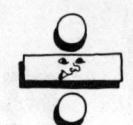

Find the following, giving your answers in their lowest terms:

1. $\frac{2}{3} \div 4$
2. $\frac{9}{11} \div 3$
3. $\frac{10}{21} \div 5$
4. $\frac{14}{19} \div 7$
5. $1\frac{1}{2} \div 3$

6. $1\frac{1}{4} \div 5$
7. $3\frac{3}{7} \div 8$
8. $2\frac{2}{5} \div 6$
9. $\frac{7}{12} \div \frac{3}{4}$
10. $\frac{3}{8} \div \frac{1}{4}$

11. $\frac{4}{15} \div \frac{1}{5}$
12. $\frac{7}{16} \div \frac{1}{8}$
13. $12 \div \frac{1}{3}$
14. $14 \div \frac{7}{9}$
15. $18 \div \frac{9}{10}$

16. $6 \div \frac{12}{17}$
17. $\frac{9}{16} \div \frac{3}{4}$
18. $\frac{3}{7} \div \frac{3}{4}$
19. $\frac{7}{9} \div \frac{14}{27}$
20. $\frac{4}{13} \div \frac{5}{26}$

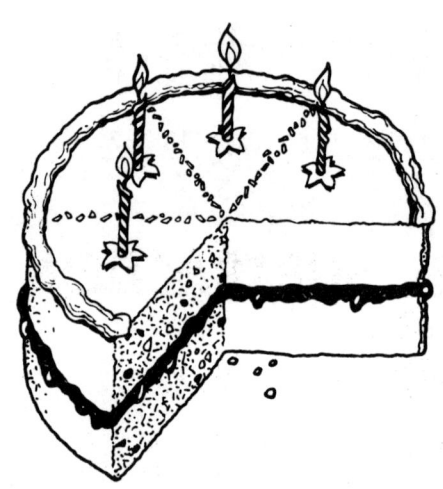

7 FURTHER FRACTIONS

A. ADDITION

Give your answers in their lowest terms:

1. $2\frac{1}{2} + 3\frac{1}{2}$
2. $3\frac{3}{4} + 4\frac{1}{4}$
3. $5\frac{3}{10} + 2\frac{1}{10}$
4. $3\frac{1}{5} + 2\frac{3}{5}$
5. $5\frac{7}{10} + 2\frac{9}{10}$

6. $4\frac{1}{8} + 2\frac{3}{8}$
7. $4\frac{5}{7} + 3\frac{3}{7}$
8. $8\frac{3}{8} + 4\frac{7}{8}$
9. $3\frac{1}{2} + 2\frac{1}{4}$
10. $3\frac{1}{2} + 1\frac{3}{4}$

11. $5\frac{1}{6} + 4\frac{1}{3}$
12. $3\frac{5}{12} + 4\frac{1}{2}$
13. $4\frac{1}{7} + 1\frac{1}{5}$
14. $6\frac{7}{9} + 5\frac{1}{2}$
15. $2\frac{4}{7} + 3\frac{2}{5}$

16. $4\frac{2}{5} + 3\frac{4}{15}$
17. $4\frac{1}{2} + 2\frac{1}{4} + 1\frac{3}{4}$
18. $3\frac{2}{15} + \frac{1}{5} + \frac{3}{10}$
19. $3\frac{6}{7} + 4\frac{1}{2} + \frac{3}{4}$
20. $5\frac{7}{12} + 6\frac{2}{3} + \frac{4}{5}$

B. SUBTRACTION

21. $2\frac{3}{4} - 1\frac{1}{4}$
22. $4\frac{7}{8} - 1\frac{5}{8}$
23. $9\frac{2}{3} - 5\frac{1}{3}$
24. $5\frac{5}{6} - \frac{1}{6}$
25. $8\frac{7}{12} - 6\frac{5}{12}$

26. $7\frac{4}{7} - 3\frac{3}{7}$
27. $5\frac{2}{3} - 2\frac{1}{2}$
28. $4\frac{5}{6} - 1\frac{2}{3}$
29. $2\frac{3}{4} - 1\frac{1}{2}$
30. $3\frac{5}{8} - 1\frac{7}{8}$

31. $4\frac{1}{6} - 2\frac{5}{6}$
32. $10\frac{1}{3} - 5\frac{2}{3}$
33. $6\frac{3}{7} - 3\frac{4}{7}$
34. $5\frac{5}{12} - 1\frac{7}{12}$
35. $8\frac{3}{4} - 5\frac{2}{5}$

36. $7\frac{2}{3} - 4\frac{7}{8}$
37. $7\frac{2}{9} - 4\frac{5}{6}$
38. $6\frac{5}{8} - 1\frac{7}{12}$
39. $9\frac{3}{7} - 2\frac{4}{5}$
40. $10\frac{1}{4} - 3\frac{4}{5}$

C. MULTIPLICATION

41. $\frac{3}{8} \times 4$ 46. $3\frac{1}{3} \times 2\frac{2}{5}$ 51. $4\frac{7}{9} \times \frac{9}{19}$ 56. $2\frac{2}{3} \times 2\frac{1}{4}$

42. $\frac{3}{4} \times 2$ 47. $2\frac{2}{11} \times 1\frac{3}{8}$ 52. $8\frac{4}{5} \times \frac{5}{11}$ 57. $1\frac{3}{4} \times 2\frac{2}{3}$

43. $10 \times 2\frac{1}{2}$ 48. $5\frac{1}{2} \times 1\frac{3}{11}$ 53. $2\frac{1}{2} \times 1\frac{7}{10}$ 58. $3\frac{1}{3} \times 4\frac{1}{5}$

44. $5 \times \frac{7}{10}$ 49. $4\frac{2}{3} \times \frac{3}{7}$ 54. $3\frac{1}{5} \times 1\frac{1}{4}$ 59. $6\frac{4}{5} \times 1\frac{8}{17}$

45. $1\frac{1}{3} \times 1\frac{1}{4}$ 50. $2\frac{1}{4} \times \frac{2}{9}$ 55. $4\frac{2}{7} \times 2\frac{1}{3}$ 60. $3\frac{1}{9} \times 1\frac{2}{7} \times \frac{3}{4}$

D. DIVISION

61. $1\frac{1}{2} \div 4\frac{1}{2}$ 66. $5\frac{1}{3} \div 1\frac{3}{5}$ 71. $1\frac{5}{7} \div 1\frac{1}{7}$ 76. $6\frac{2}{3} \div 2\frac{6}{7}$

62. $3\frac{1}{3} \div 2\frac{6}{7}$ 67. $4\frac{2}{7} \div 1\frac{3}{7}$ 72. $2\frac{2}{5} \div 3\frac{3}{5}$ 77. $8\frac{4}{7} \div 6\frac{2}{3}$

63. $3\frac{1}{2} \div 6\frac{1}{8}$ 68. $1\frac{3}{4} \div 1\frac{7}{8}$ 73. $3\frac{1}{7} \div 3\frac{2}{3}$ 78. $9\frac{1}{7} \div 5\frac{1}{3}$

64. $7\frac{1}{3} \div 1\frac{5}{6}$ 69. $1\frac{1}{3} \div 1\frac{1}{7}$ 74. $1\frac{1}{3} \div 2\frac{4}{9}$ 79. $7\frac{3}{7} \div 1\frac{6}{7}$

65. $4\frac{1}{5} \div 1\frac{2}{5}$ 70. $3\frac{3}{8} \div 2\frac{1}{4}$ 75. $5\frac{1}{7} \div 2\frac{2}{5}$ 80. $10\frac{2}{3} \div 2\frac{10}{27}$

8 DECIMALS

A. ADDITION

1. 0.2 + 0.3
2. 0.4 + 0.5
3. 0.3 + 0.6
4. 1.4 + 2.5
5. 2.6 + 7.1
6. 6.2 + 3.7
7. 3.7 + 2.4
8. 5.5 + 2.6
9. 7.9 + 1.2
10. 5.6 + 4.5
11. 3.9 + 6.4
12. 8.2 + 5.9
13. 6.4 + 8.2
14. 5.3 + 7.4
15. 8.5 + 9.3
16. 15.2 + 8.4
17. 26.7 + 6.2
18. 7.9 + 4.7
19. 8.6 + 9.5
20. 22.6 + 19.9

B. SUBTRACTION

1. 0.9 − 0.5
2. 0.8 − 0.6
3. 0.7 − 0.3
4. 1.4 − 0.1
5. 2.8 − 0.5
6. 3.7 − 1.6
7. 5.9 − 2.8
8. 7.9 − 5.2
9. 3.8 − 2.5
10. 1.5 − 0.6
11. 1.7 − 0.9
12. 2.3 − 0.4
13. 2.6 − 0.8
14. 3.4 − 1.5
15. 4.6 − 2.8
16. 5.7 − 3.9
17. 16.4 − 9.2
18. 24.2 − 16.1
19. 34.3 − 26.7
20. 50 − 23.7

C. MULTIPLICATION BY 10

Multiply the following numbers by 10:

1. 4.7 × 10 = 47

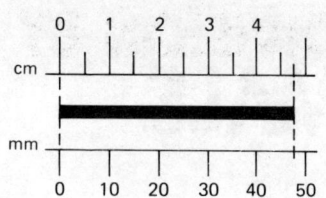

2. 5.3	5. 1.4	8. 7.46
3. 8.6	6. 9.3	9. 59.2
4. 3.9	7. 12.3	10. 34.7

D. MULTIPLICATION BY 100

Multiply the following numbers by 100:

1. $7.3 \times 100 = 730$

2. 4.1	7. 28.4
3. 16.1	8. 63.2
4. 3.92	9. 44
5. 4.41	10. 8.74
6. 8.67	11. 1.728

E. MULTIPLICATION

1. 0.4×2	9. 0.9×7	17. 6.2×5	25. 6.9×5.2
2. 0.3×2	10. 0.3×5	18. 8.1×6	26. 9.3×7.6
3. 0.6×2	11. 0.4×8	19. 9.2×7	27. 5.1×7.2
4. 0.4×3	12. 0.7×9	20. 4.4×8	28. 8.8×4.7
5. 0.6×3	13. 1.2×3	21. 2.4×1.2	29. 9.8×6.3
6. 0.8×3	14. 2.3×2	22. 3.6×4.3	30. 6.7×7.6
7. 0.7×4	15. 4.1×3	23. 5.6×4.7	31. 4.9×8.5
8. 0.8×5	16. 5.3×4	24. 8.2×3.1	32. 12.4×6.7

F. DIVISION BY 10

Divide the following numbers by 10:

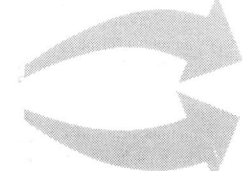

1. 54 ÷ 10 = 5.4

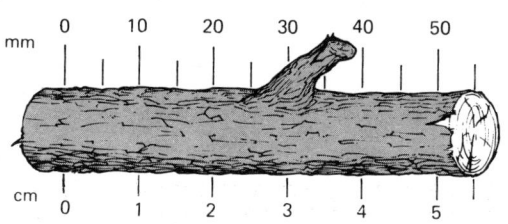

2. 36	5. 6.3	8. 54.5	
3. 79	6. 4.7	9. 16.2	
4. 8.2	7. 41.6	10. 525	

G. DIVISION BY 100

Divide the following numbers by 100:

1. 342 ÷ 100 = 3.42

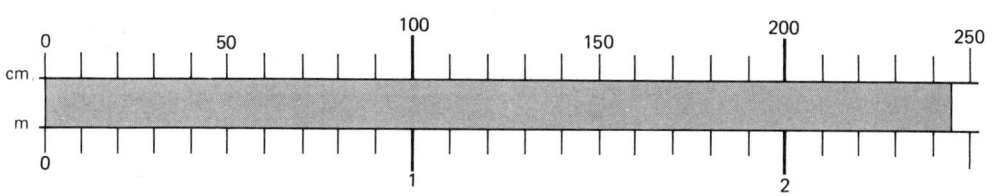

2. 726   7. 1.73
3. 145   8. 4.26
4. 84.4 9. 6300
5. 36.2 10. 8140
6. 58.7

H. DIVISION

Find:

 **1.** $2.1 \div 3 = 0.7$

2. $1.6 \div 4$	9. $0.63 \div 9$	16. $11.7 \div 1.3$	23. $2.24 \div 0.4$
3. $6.5 \div 5$	10. $0.42 \div 7$	17. $16.5 \div 5.5$	24. $3.04 \div 0.8$
4. $4.8 \div 4$	11. $3.6 \div 1.2$	18. $58.8 \div 8.4$	25. $3.24 \div 0.36$
5. $8.6 \div 2$	12. $11.5 \div 2.3$	19. $23.8 \div 3.4$	26. $5.18 \div 0.74$
6. $7.7 \div 7$	13. $20.5 \div 4.1$	20. $60.8 \div 7.6$	27. $1.176 \div 0.56$
7. $0.72 \div 8$	14. $17 \div 3.4$	21. $1.47 \div 0.7$	28. $3.645 \div 0.81$
8. $0.24 \div 6$	15. $52 \div 6.5$	22. $1.3 \div 0.5$	29. $3.484 \div 0.67$

9 FRACTIONS AND DECIMALS

Convert the following fractions into decimals.
Give any answers which are not exact correct to 3 figures:

1. $\frac{1}{4} = 0.25$

2. $\frac{3}{5} = 0.6$

3. $\frac{3}{4}$
4. $\frac{2}{5}$
5. $\frac{3}{10}$
6. $\frac{7}{10}$
7. $\frac{17}{50}$
8. $\frac{47}{50}$
9. $\frac{7}{20}$
10. $\frac{19}{20}$
11. $\frac{3}{8}$
12. $\frac{7}{8}$
13. $\frac{1}{3}$
14. $\frac{2}{3}$
15. $\frac{5}{6}$
16. $\frac{7}{12}$
17. $1\frac{3}{4}$
18. $2\frac{1}{2}$
19. $3\frac{3}{8}$
20. $4\frac{4}{5}$

Convert the following decimals into fractions in their lowest terms:

21. $0.3 = \frac{3}{10}$

22. $0.45 = \frac{45}{100} = \frac{9}{20}$

23. $0.625 = \frac{625}{1000} = \frac{25}{40} = \frac{5}{8}$

24. 0.8
25. 0.7
26. 0.2
27. 0.9
28. 0.75
29. 0.65
30. 0.25
31. 0.85
32. 0.72
33. 0.48
34. 0.16
35. 0.64
36. 0.26
37. 0.38
38. 0.79
39. 0.41
40. 0.53

10 NEGATIVE NUMBERS

Simplify:

1. $12 - 6 = 6$
2. $5 - 10 = -5$
3. $4 + (-5) = -1$
4. $8 - (-5) = 13$

5. $8 - 4$
6. $3 - 6$
7. $3 + (-7)$
8. $4 - (-7)$
9. $6 - 10$
10. $12 - 4$
11. $-10 + 6$
12. $-10 - 6$
13. $-5 - 4$
14. $-8 + 3$
15. $5 + (-2)$
16. $5 - (-2)$
17. $13 + (-5)$
18. $12 - (-5)$
19. $7 + (-10)$
20. $7 - (-6)$
21. $-4 + (-3)$
22. $-4 + (-6)$

23. $-2 - (-7)$
24. $-5 - (-12)$
25. $-6 - (-8)$
26. $-5 + (-3)$
27. $-6 + (-8)$
28. $8 - 12$
29. $-14 - 2$
30. $0 + (-5)$
31. $0 - (-8)$
32. $0 - (-7)$
33. $0 + (-10)$
34. $9 + (-3)$
35. $10 - (-4)$
36. $-8 + (-10)$
37. $-7 - (-3)$
38. $-18 - (-8)$
39. $-15 + (-10)$
40. $-5 - 10$

I am on the 8th floor of a block of flats:

41. If I go down 5 floors where am I?
42. If I go up 3 floors where am I?
43. If I go down 9 floors where am I?

The temperature outside is 6°C:

44. If it goes up 10°C what is the new temperature?
45. If it goes down 10°C what is the new temperature?

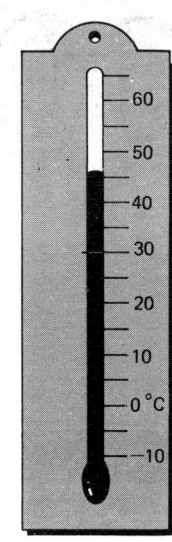

11 APPROXIMATIONS, DECIMAL PLACES, STANDARD FORM, SIGNIFICANT FIGURES

Express these numbers correct to the nearest 10:

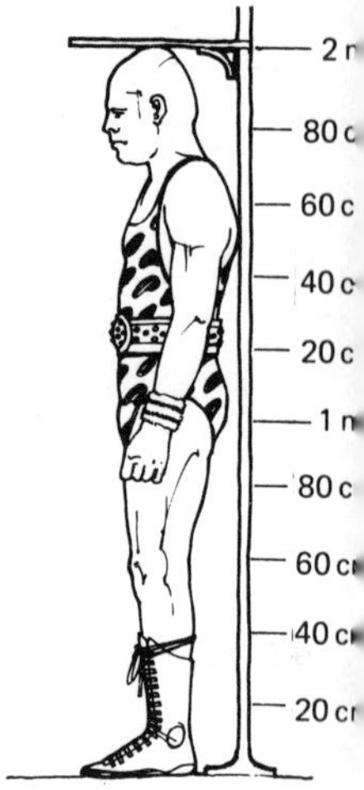

1. 644 → 640
2. 1867 → 1870

3. 3978
4. 134
5. 76
6. 284
7. 397
8. 2455
9. 5766
10. 444
11. 137
12. 254
13. 88

Express these numbers correct to the nearest 100:

14. 6540 → 6500
15. 1493 → 1500

16. 2283
17. 5276
18. 349
19. 789
20. 7264
21. 504
22. 856
23. 2567
24. 11 592
25. 6953

Express these numbers correct to the nearest 1000:

26. 7200 → 7000
27. 13 643 → 14 000

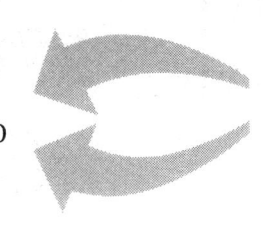

28. 2400
29. 6800
30. 15 920
31. 3340
32. 8686
33. 43 894
34. 954
35. 1288
36. 37 782
37. 21 439

Express these numbers correct to
(a) 1 decimal place, (b) 2 decimal places:

38. 14.6565 → (a) 14.7 (b) 14.66
39. 264.0972 → (a) 264.1 (b) 264.10

40. 4.747
41. 8.334
42. 0.559
43. 4.732
44. 6.489
45. 27.821
46. 18.145
47. 25.554
48. 345.077
49. 436.828

Express these numbers correct to
(a) 1 decimal place, (b) 3 decimal places:

50. 72.4453 → (a) 72.4 (b) 72.445
51. 137.9247 → (a) 137.9 (b) 137.925

52. 1.4936
53. 5.0384
54. 6.3976
55. 44.5555
56. 0.0973
57. 0.8439
58. 0.0077
59. 8.7474
60. 3.4949
61. 122.6666

Express these numbers correct to the nearest whole number:

62. 58.6 → 59
63. 126.043 → 126

64. 44.4
65. 62.6
66. 1.84

67. 7.26
68. 18.49
69. 26.59

70. 154.66
71. 0.954
72. 474.7

73. 98.09

Express these numbers correct to 2 significant figures:

74. 6.84 → 6.8
75. 149.6 → 150

76. 4780
77. 68.7
78. 16.9

79. 4.44
80. 7.432
81. 368

82. 833
83. 37.48
84. 0.747

85. 0.08664
86. 8.008
87. 1589

Express these numbers correct to 3 significant figures:

88. 57.264 → 57.3
89. 672.944 → 673
90. 0.048 774 → 0.0488

91. 15.47
92. 5.925
93. 7266

94. 38.94
95. 1.178
96. 16742

97. 2898
98. 0.044 44
99. 0.3947

100. 68.97

Express these numbers in standard form:

101. $4300 = 4.3 \times 1000 = 4.3 \times 10^3$

102. $672.4 = 6.724 \times 100$
   $= 6.724 \times 10^2$

103. $0.0092 = 9.2 \times \frac{1}{1000}$
   $= \frac{9.2}{10^3} = 9.2 \times 10^{-3}$

104. 7600
105. 476
106. 268

107. 9380
108. 54300
109. 86 000

110. 11.92
111. 46.07
112. 0.042

113. 0.0684
114. 0.0049
115. 0.000 82

The attendances for five first division matches one Saturday last season are given below, correct to the nearest 1000. In each case state (a) the maximum possible attendance, (b) the minimum possible attendance:

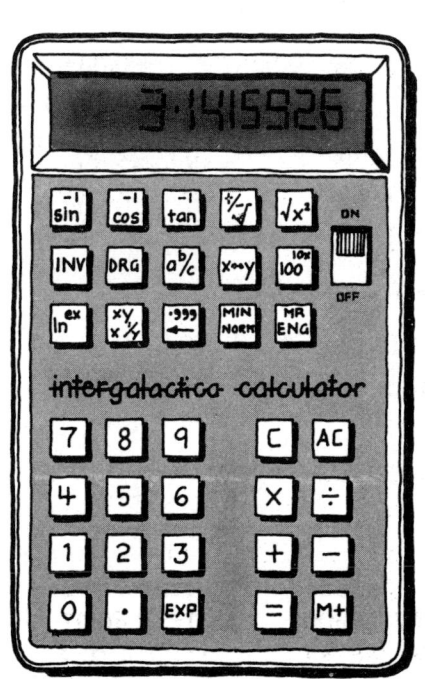

		maximum number	*minimum number*
116.	47 000	47 499	46 500

117. 10 000
118. 23 000
119. 37 000
120. 15 000

NEWTOWN F.C. ELECTRA SCORE

	ATTENDANCE	FINAL SCORE
LAST WEEK	34 760	5 - 3
TODAY	36 569	0 - 0

These numbers occurred on the displays of various calculators. Give each number correct to 4 significant figures:

121. 2.1464537 → 2.146
122. 0.009 267 68 → 0.009 268
123. 4.927 64   09 → 4 928 000 000
124. 3.644 65   −08 → 0.000 000 036 45

125. 923.542 36
126. 15.249 092
127. 0.474 747 4
128. 0.007 177 7
129. 0.0921536
130. 3.1427   06
131. 7.3499   05
132. 8.2492   07
133. 2.2466   −09
134. 5.0088   −04
135. 6.5007   −10

12 MONEY

Write each of the following in pounds:

1. £1 and 60 pence = £1.60

2. £3 and 40 pence
3. £2 and 70 pence
4. £3 and 76 pence
5. £4 and 25 pence
6. £5 and 39 pence

7. £7 and 83 pence
8. £2 and 6 pence
9. £3 and 8 pence
10. £10 and 50 pence

Write each of the following in pence:

11. £0.50 = 50p
12. £0.07 = 7p

13. £0.70
14. £0.90
15. £0.25
16. £0.66
17. £0.48
18. £0.33
19. £0.82
20. £0.96

21. £1.36 = 136p

22. £1.42
23. £1.65
24. £3.64
25. £4.13
26. £8.50
27. £9.72
28. £3.34
29. £12.40
30. £15.72

Read the following amounts as you would expect to hear them in everyday use:

31. £3.40   Three pounds forty
32. £0.75   Seventy-five pence

33. £1.50
34. £2.70
35. £8.30
36. £1.34
37. £2.63
38. £4.19
39. £0.25
40. £0.40
41. £0.78
42. £0.16
43. £0.27
44. £0.69
45. £20.56
46. £52.99
47. £80.12
48. £50.08
49. £27.45
50. £120.75

Write each of the following in figures:

51. Thirty-seven pence = 37p

52. Fifty-two pence
53. Seventy pence
54. Ninety-two pence
55. Forty-four pence
56. One hundred and seven pence
    = 107p
57. Two hundred and twenty pence
58. One hundred and nine pence
59. Five hundred and fifty-six pence
60. Eight hundred and seven pence

Write each of the following in pounds:

61. Fifty-six pence = £0.56

62. Forty-three pence
63. Eighty pence
64. Sixteen pence
65. Twenty-one pence
66. Three pounds forty-six pence
  = £3.46
67. Two pounds twenty pence
68. Nine pounds eighteen pence
69. Seven pounds thirty-four pence
70. Eight pounds and four pence
71. Sixteen pounds sixteen pence
72. Thirty-six pounds seventy-two pence
73. Fifty-seven pounds twenty = £57.20
74. Forty pounds thirty-three
75. Sixty-four pounds fifty
76. Twelve pounds forty-four
77. Three pounds sixteen
78. Nine pounds twelve
79. One hundred and four pounds ten
80. Two hundred and thirty-three pounds fifty-four

13 MONEY — THE FOUR RULES

In this exercise you may use a calculator.

A. ADDITION

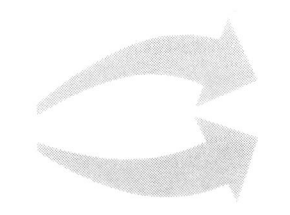

1.   p
   42
   36
   ―
   78

or if a calculator is used:

| AC | 4 | 2 |
| + | 3 | 6 | = | 78p |

2.   p
   32
   55
   ―

3.   p
   74
   13
   ―

4.   p
   55
   23
   ―

5.   £
   0.47
   0.16
   ―

6.   £
   0.56
   0.28
   ―

7.   £
   0.67
   0.58
   ―

8.   £
   0.28
   0.83
   ―

9.   £
   0.14
   0.53
   0.31
   ―

10. £
   0.22
   0.33
   0.44
   ___

11. £
   0.51
   0.13
   0.25
   ___

12. £
   0.24
   0.42
   0.13
   ___

13. £
   0.64
   0.16
   ___

14. £
   0.42
   0.18
   ___

15. £
   0.72
   0.39
   ___

16. £
   0.66
   0.57
   ___

17. £
   0.62
   0.17
   0.18
   ___

18. £
   0.11
   0.49
   0.27
   ___

19. £
   0.36
   0.45
   0.82
   ___

20. £
   0.73
   0.54
   0.19
   ___

21. £
   0.99
   0.17
   0.74
   ___

22. £
   1.26
   3.45
   5.17
   ___
   9.88

or [AC] [1] [.] [2] [6] [+] [3] [.] [4] [5] [+] [5] [.] [1] [7] [=] £9.88

23. £
   6.17
   0.45
   1.37
   ___

24. £
   2.23
   1.64
   2.88
   ___

25. £
   3.51
   4.73
   1.98
   ___

26. £
   7.64
   3.92
   1.66
   ___

27. £
   3.35
   8.26
   4.17
   ___

28. £
   12.92
   30.43
   8.26
   ___

29. £
   18.61
   4.95
   33.17
   3.52
   ___

30. £
   16.44
   3.54
   40.02
   18.61
   ___

31. £
   34.02
   9.16
   18.44
   16.09
   ___

32. £
   12.43
   8.04
   9.16
   24.27
   ___

33. £
   34.62
   138.90
   57.02
   228.17
   ___

34. £
   216.40
   159.73
   47.25
   386.74
   ___

B. SUBTRACTION

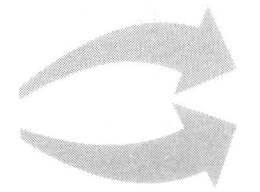

1. p
    84   or | AC | 8 | 4 |
    13 | − | 1 | 3 | = 71p
    —
    71

2. p
    59
    37
    —

3. p
    87
    43
    —

4. p
    56
    44
    —

5. p
    72
    63
    —

6. p
    84
    15
    —

7. p
    53
    27
    —

8. p
    65
    39
    —

9. £
    0.66
    0.34
    —

10. £
    0.79
    0.27
    —

11. £
    0.68
    0.17
    —

12. £
    0.89
    0.35
    —

13. £
    0.53
    0.24
    —

14. £
    0.65
    0.48
    —

15. £
    0.71
    0.59
    —

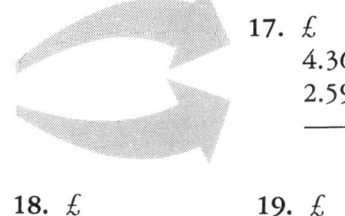

16. £
    0.47
    0.28
    —

17. £   or | AC | 4 | . | 3 | 6 |
    4.36 | − | 2 | . | 5 | 9 |
    2.59 | = | £1.77 |
    —

18. £
    3.27
    1.89
    —

19. £
    5.54
    3.88
    —

20. £
    12.25
    9.42
    —

21. £
    26.38
    7.43
    —

22. £
   34.46
   18.55

23. £
   40.35
   8.72

24. £
   34.29
   17.73

25. £
   44.53
   18.76

26. £
   50.26
   22.57

27. £
   85.34
   8.67

28. £
   54.17
   18.69

29. £
   98.44
   39.87

30. £
   137.20
   92.66

31. £
   247.85
   78.47

32. £
   339.36
   183.67

33. £
   241.61
   88.43

34. £
   446.73
   249.16

35. £
   517.26
   348.92

36. £
   217.09
   164.73

37. £
   413.91
   387.27

C. MULTIPLICATION

Multiply:

1. 12p by 3
2. 22p by 4
3. 33p by 3
4. £1.21 by 3
5. £2.12 by 4
6. £1.36 by 4
7. £2.40 by 10
8. £1.62 by 10
9. £1.43 by 4
10. £3.20 by 5
11. £4.16 by 5
12. £5.24 by 5
13. £2.34 by 6
14. £5.72 by 6
15. £8.13 by 6

16. £ 4.14   or
        7× | AC | 4 | . | 1 | 4 |
       ─────
       £28.98 | × | 7 | = | £28.98 |

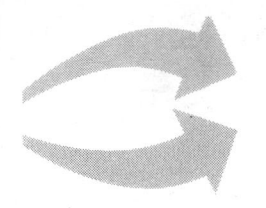

17. £7.13 by 8
18. £5.73 by 7
19. £34.20 by 10
20. £42.14 by 4
21. £18.36 by 4

22. £26.35 by 5
23. £60.24 by 5
24. £37.61 by 5
25. £48.33 by 6
26. £29.25 by 7

27. £52.67 by 8
28. £34.03 by 7
29. £40.27 by 8
30. £19.23 by 9
31. £15.44 by 9

32. £24.47 by 9
33. £37.37 by 7
34. £124.30 by 5
35. £214.88 by 6
36. £87.52 by 8

D. DIVISION

Divide:

1. 36p by 2
2. 84p by 4
3. 64p by 4

4. 276p by 3
5. 125p by 5
6. 294p by 7

7. 363p by 3
8. 164p by 4
9. 575p by 5

10. £1.20 by 4
11. £4.25 by 5
12. £7.92 by 6

13. £4.98 by 6

    0.83   or | AC | 4 | . | 9 | 8 |
  6)4.98
                   | ÷ | 6 | = | £0.83 or 83p |
  i.e. 83p

14. £6.81 by 3
15. £5.46 by 7
16. £2.56 by 8
17. £6.64 by 8
18. £9.92 by 8
19. £8.65 by 5

20. £6.84 by 6
21. £15.12 by 7
22. £14.45 by 5
23. £26 by 8
24. £7.92 by 9
25. £45.80 by 10

26. £37.90 by 10
27. £12.54 by 11
28. £120.80 by 20
29. £123.45 by 15
30. £92.88 by 12
31. £34.56 by 18

32. £56 by 100
33. £33.93 by 13
34. £36.96 by 24
35. £75.52 by 32
36. £54.06 by 17
37. £134.82 by 21

14 SHOPPING

Prices shown: Peas 46p lb; Swedes 18p lb; Apples 32p lb; Bananas 52p lb; Oranges 14p each; Beans 86p lb; Cauli's 50p each; Tomatoes 64p lb; Parsnips 15p lb; Potatoes 18p lb; Carrots 32p lb.

Use the information given above to find the cost of:

1. 2 lb carrots
2. 5 lb potatoes
3. 3 lb beans
4. 2 lb parsnips
5. 6 oranges
6. 4 lb apples
7. 2 lb swedes
8. 3 lb bananas
9. $1\frac{1}{2}$ lb peas
10. $3\frac{1}{2}$ lb carrots
11. $2\frac{1}{2}$ lb swedes
12. 8 lb potatoes
13. 2 cauliflowers
14. $1\frac{1}{2}$ lb tomatoes
15. 9 lb potatoes
16. 9 oranges
17. 5 lb apples
18. 5 lb carrots
19. 4 lb bananas
20. 3 lb parsnips

Copy and complete these shopping lists. How much change would there be in each case from a £10 note?

21. 3 lb carrots
    2 lb parsnips
    6 lb potatoes
    _____

22. 6 oranges
    2 lb bananas
    4 lb apples
    _____

23. 3 lb tomatoes
    3 lb bananas
    7 oranges   _____

24. 3 lb carrots
    7 lb potatoes
    3 lb swedes   _____

25. 2 lb carrots
    3 lb parsnips
    2 lb swedes
    1 cauliflower   _____

26. 3 lb apples
    2 lb tomatoes
    5 oranges
    3 lb peas   _____

Use the information given above to find the cost of:

27. 5 kg potatoes
28. 2 kg parsnips
29. 1 kg peas
30. 3 kg cabbage
31. 5 swedes
32. $1\frac{1}{2}$ kg carrots

Copy and complete these shopping lists. How much change would there be in each case from a £10 note?

33. 2 kg carrots
    2 kg parsnips
    7 kg potatoes   _____

34. $1\frac{1}{2}$ kg peas
    1 kg cabbage
    3 swedes   _____

35. $\frac{1}{2}$ kg carrots
    1 kg parsnips
    2 kg potatoes
    1 swede   _____

36. $2\frac{1}{2}$ kg carrots
    2 kg parsnips
    3 kg potatoes
    $1\frac{1}{2}$ kg peas   _____

Use your calculator to find the totals for the following supermarket bills:

37.	0.22	40.	0.54	42.	0.53	44.	0.55
	0.22		0.62		0.46		0.43
	0.34		0.45		0.72		0.27
	0.14		0.27		0.16		0.36
	0.16		0.27		0.52		0.82
	0.78		0.27		0.52		0.73
	0.44		0.51		0.76		0.92
	0.37		1.63		1.34		0.64
	1.26		1.74		0.86		0.53
	0.84		2.92		0.73		0.44
	———		0.33		1.06		0.67
			0.35		0.86		0.59
			0.35		0.43		0.22
			0.62		1.17		0.22
			0.45		0.93		0.22
38.	0.88		0.72		0.32		0.22
	0.64		0.85		0.47		———
	0.72		———		0.55		
	0.69				———		
	0.32						
	0.32						
	0.32						
	0.32						
	0.75	41.	3.41	43.	0.27	45.	3.46
	0.61		0.67		0.27		0.82
	0.77		0.23		0.27		0.16
	0.26		0.47		0.38		0.18
	0.26		0.36		0.88		0.19
	———		0.28		0.65		0.23
			0.45		0.52		0.45
			0.88		0.18		0.62
			0.75		0.27		1.74
			0.26		0.53		0.93
39.	1.27		0.38		0.44		0.39
	0.81		0.38		0.44		0.42
	0.44		2.47		1.26		———
	0.44		1.93		0.44		
	0.13		3.42		0.27		
	0.27		4.50		0.29		
	1.61		0.62		0.86		
	4.29		0.74		———		
	3.17		0.82				
	0.45		0.74				
	0.37		0.62				
	0.82		0.31				
	0.66		0.31				
	———		———				

SCROOGE
accountants Ltd.

BOB CRATCHIT'S BILL

0.44
1.62
0.16
0.47
0.53
3.41
0.27
0.34
1.61
0.10
1.26
0.62
0.33
1.74
0.18
0.82
0.59
2.15½
1.34
0.00½
0.93
4.50

15 METRIC QUANTITIES

A. LENGTH

Measure each of the given straight lines to the nearest centimetre (cm):

1. _____   4. _____

2. _____   5. _____

3. _____

Measure each of the following straight lines correct to the nearest millimetre (mm):

6. _____   9. _____

7. _____   10. _____

8. _____

Draw straight lines of length:

11. 8 cm   14. 8.5 cm
12. 14 cm   15. 6.8 cm
13. 12 cm

Draw straight lines of length:

16. 64 mm   19. 154 mm
17. 89 mm   20. 93 mm
18. 132 mm

41

Convert:

21. 5 km into metres:
    5 km = 5 × 1000 m
        = 5000 m

22. 14 km into m
23. 8.24 km into m
24. 3.93 km into m
25. 0.726 km into m

26. 2.4 m into centimetres: 2.4 m = 2.4 × 100 cm = 240 cm

27. 5.5 m into cm
28. 7.8 m into cm
29. 0.92 m into cm
30. 0.536 m into cm

31. 50 cm into millimetres: 50 cm = 50 × 10 mm = 500 mm

32. 44 cm into mm
33. 126 cm into mm
34. 82.6 cm into mm
35. 6.34 cm into mm

36. 3500 m into kilometres: 3500 m = 3500 ÷ 1000 km = 3.5 km

37. 7000 m into km
38. 9630 m into km
39. 15 800 m into km
40. 247 m into km

41. 624 cm into metres: 624 cm = 624 ÷ 100 m = 6.24 m

42. 347 cm into m
43. 1593 cm into m
44. 43 cm into m
45. 6.29 cm into m

46. 540 mm into centimetres: 540 mm = 540 ÷ 10 cm = 54 cm

47. 820 mm into cm
48. 2730 mm into cm
49. 46 mm into cm
50. 127.3 mm into cm

B. AREA

Change:

1. 5 cm^2 into mm^2:
   5 cm^2 = 5 × 100 mm^2
          = 500 mm^2

2. 12 cm^2 into mm^2
3. 20 cm^2 into mm^2
4. 0.75 cm^2 into mm^2
5. 1.64 cm^2 into mm^2

6. 1.5 m² into cm²: 1.5 m² = 1.5 × 10 000 cm² = 15 000 cm²
7. 0.5 m² into cm²
8. 0.4 m² into cm²
9. 0.36 m² into cm²
10. 0.03 m² into cm²

11. 3 km² into hectares (ha):   3 km² = 3 × 100 ha = 300 ha
12. 5 km² into ha
13. 10 km² into ha
14. 7 km² into ha
15. 8.5 km² into ha

16. 300 mm² into cm²: 300 mm² = 300 ÷ 100 cm² = 3 cm²
17. 500 mm² into cm²
18. 800 mm² into cm²
19. 1200 mm² into cm²
20. 7000 mm² into cm²

21. 7500 cm² into m²: 7500 cm² = 7500 ÷ 10 000 m² = 0.75 m²
22. 120 000 cm² into m²
23. 300 000 cm² into m²
24. 55 000 cm² into m²
25. 24 300 cm² into m²

26. 800 ha into km²: 800 ha = 800 ÷ 100 km² = 8 km²
27. 300 ha into km²
28. 1000 ha into km²
29. 5000 ha into km²
30. 12 000 ha into km²

C. VOLUME (CAPACITY)

Change

1. 3 litres into cm³:
   3 litres = 3 × 1000 cm³
            = 3000 cm³

2. 8 litres into cm³
3. 12 litres into cm³
4. 1.5 litres into cm³
5. 0.5 litres into cm³

6. 500 cm³ into litres: 500 cm³ = 500 ÷ 1000 litres = 0.5 litres

7. 2000 cm³ into litres
8. 6000 cm³ into litres
9. 400 cm³ into litres
10. 70 cm³ into litres

D. WEIGHT (MASS)

Change:

1. 3 kg into g:
   3 kg = 3 × 1000 g
        = 3000 g

2. 7 kg into g
3. 4.5 kg into g
4. 0.27 kg into g
5. 0.146 kg into g

6. 4 tonnes (t) into kilograms: 4 t = 4 × 1000 kg = 4000 kg

7. 9 t into kg
8. 1.3 t into kg
9. 0.75 t into kg
10. 0.025 t into kg

11. 9000 g into kilograms: 9000 g = 9000 ÷ 1000 kg = 9 kg

12. 4000 g into kg
13. 12 000 g into kg
14. 800 g into kg
15. 250 g into kg

16. 6000 kg into tonnes: 6000 kg = 6000 ÷ 1000 t = 6 t

17. 5000 kg into t
18. 7500 kg into t
19. 500 kg into t
20. 10 000 kg into t

16 PERCENTAGES

Convert the given decimals into percentages:

1. $0.8 = 0.8 \times 100\% = 80\%$
2. $0.45 = 0.45 \times 100\% = 45\%$

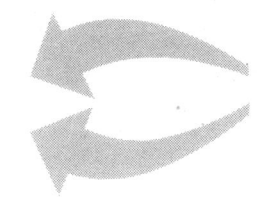

3. 0.5
4. 0.25
5. 0.75
6. 0.6
7. 0.3

8. 0.55
9. 0.85
10. 0.48
11. 0.37
12. 0.12

13. 0.69
14. 1.24
15. 1.53
16. 2.64
17. 0.05

18. 0.09
19. 0.88
20. 0.43
21. 3.24
22. 1.72

Convert the given fractions into percentages:

23. $\frac{1}{2} = \frac{1}{2} \times 100\% = 50\%$

24. $\frac{5}{8} = \frac{5}{8} \times 100\% = 62.5\%$

25. $\frac{1}{4}$

26. $\frac{3}{8}$

27. $\frac{7}{8}$

28. $\frac{3}{4}$

29. $\frac{3}{5}$

30. $\frac{4}{5}$

31. $\frac{2}{5}$

32. $\frac{1}{5}$

33. $\frac{7}{20}$

34. $\frac{9}{20}$

35. $\frac{17}{20}$

36. $\frac{13}{20}$

37. $\frac{1}{3}$

38. $\frac{2}{3}$

39. $1\frac{5}{8}$

40. $1\frac{3}{8}$

41. $3\frac{1}{5}$

42. $2\frac{7}{10}$

43. $3\frac{3}{5}$

44. $1\frac{7}{8}$

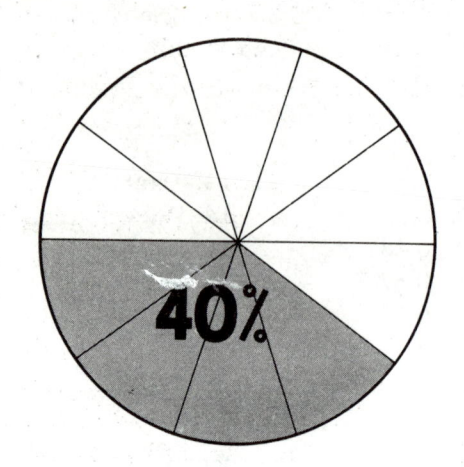

Convert the given percentages into (a) decimals, (b) fractions:

45. (a) $40\% = \frac{40}{100} = 0.4$

    (b) $40\% = \frac{40}{100} = \frac{2}{5}$

46. (a) $65\% = \frac{65}{100} = 0.65$

    (b) $65\% = \frac{65}{100} = \frac{13}{20}$

47. 10%
48. 30%
49. 25%
50. 55%
51. 85%
52. 90%
53. 64%
54. 46%
55. 95%
56. 72%
57. $33\frac{1}{3}\%$
58. $66\frac{2}{3}\%$
59. $12\frac{1}{2}\%$
60. 130%
61. 344%
62. $67\frac{1}{2}\%$
63. $56\frac{1}{4}\%$
64. $6\frac{1}{4}\%$

Express the first quantity as a percentage of the second:

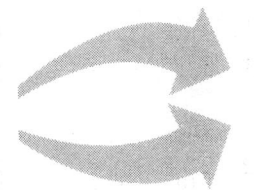

65. 4, 16: $\frac{4}{16} \times 100\% = 25\%$

66. 66 cm, 2 m: $\frac{66}{200} \times 100\% = 33\%$

67. 20, 25
68. 8, 32
69. 45, 60
70. 60, 30
71. 3 km, 8 km
72. 8 cm, 5 cm
73. 4 m, 12 m
74. 5 mm, 1 cm

Find the value of:

75. 60% of 5 cm = $5 \times \frac{60}{100}$ cm = 3 cm

76. 42% of 15 km = $15 \times \frac{42}{100}$ km
    = 6.3 km

77. 10% of 5 m
78. 20% of 35 cm
79. 30% of 44 mm
80. 70% of 3 km
81. 25% of 64 cm
82. 75% of 128 m
83. 64% of 25 km
84. 26% of 45 mm
85. 40% of 200 g
86. 90% of 30 t
87. 50% of 46 g
88. 15% of 40 kg
89. $33\frac{1}{3}\%$ of 36 kg
90. $12\frac{1}{2}\%$ of 72 t
91. $62\frac{1}{2}\%$ of 240 t
92. $66\frac{2}{3}\%$ of 9 kg
93. 130% of 450 g
94. 250% of 3 t

17 BUYING AND SELLING

In each of the following, write down the factor by which the cost price must be multiplied to give the selling price:

1. Profit 30%: Multiplying factor is

$$\frac{(100 + 30)}{100} \text{ or } \frac{130}{100}$$

2. Loss 40%: Multiplying factor is

$$\frac{(100 - 40)}{100} \text{ or } \frac{60}{100}$$

3. Profit 35%
4. Profit 50%
5. Profit 75%
6. Profit 12%
7. Loss 20%
8. Loss 50%
9. Loss 25%
10. Loss 43%

Find the selling price (SP):

11. Cost price (CP) £5, profit 30%:

$$SP = £5 \times \frac{130}{100} = £6.50$$

12. CP £10, loss 40%:

$$SP = £10 \times \frac{60}{100} = £6$$

13. CP £6, profit 60%
14. CP £20, profit 50%
15. CP £50, profit 12%
16. CP £44, profit 85%
17. CP £8, loss 30%
18. CP £20, loss 35%
19. CP £5, loss 8%
20. CP £65, loss 70%

In each of the following, write down the factor by which the selling price must be multiplied to give the cost price:

21. Profit 30%: Multiplying factor is

$$\frac{100}{(100+30)} \quad \text{or} \quad \frac{100}{130}$$

22. Loss 20%: Multiplying factor is

$$\frac{100}{(100-20)} \quad \text{or} \quad \frac{100}{80}$$

23. Profit 60%
24. Profit 50%
25. Profit 43%
26. Profit 72%
27. Loss 40%
28. Loss 50%
29. Loss 34%
30. Loss 65%

Find the cost price (CP):

31. SP £220, profit 10%:

$$CP = £220 \times \frac{100}{110} = £200$$

32. SP £27, loss 25%:

$$CP = £27 \times \frac{100}{75} = £36$$

49

33. SP £26, profit 30%
34. SP £69, profit 15%
35. SP £17.40, profit 45%
36. SP £7.31, profit 70%

37. SP £14, loss 30%
38. SP £84, loss 65%
39. SP £123, loss 18%
40. SP £203, loss 42%

In each of the following, find the percentage profit or loss:

41. CP £10, SP £12:   Profit
    = SP − CP = £12 − £10 = £2

    i.e. percentage profit

    $= \dfrac{\text{profit}}{\text{CP}} \times 100 = \dfrac{£2}{£10} \times 100$

    $= 20$

    i.e. profit = 20%

42. CP £10, SP £7:   Loss
    = CP − SP = £10 − £7 = £3

    i.e. percentage loss

    $= \dfrac{\text{loss}}{\text{CP}} \times 100 = \dfrac{£3}{£10} \times 100 = 30$

    i.e. loss = 30%

43. CP £4, profit £1
44. CP £25, profit £10
45. CP £12, loss £3
46. CP £40, loss £8

47. CP £60, SP £72
48. CP £80, SP £60
49. CP £24, SP £16
50. CP £16, SP £20.80

51. This year Loxforth School has 840 pupils. Next year this number is expected to increase by 15%. How many pupils do they expect to have next year? How many more classes will this give in the school if each class has 21 pupils?
52. A secondhand car dealer buys a car for £4225 and sells it at a gain of 20%. Find the selling price.
53. John buys a motorcycle for £1250 and sells it eighteen months later for £825. Find his loss per cent.
54. Anne sees a dress she likes in a shop window marked £56. In a sale all prices are reduced by 15%. How much would be saved if she waited for the sale?
55. Susan buys a British Commemorative stamp for £64 and is able to sell it 5 years later for £80. Find her percentage profit.

18 RATIO AND PROPORTION

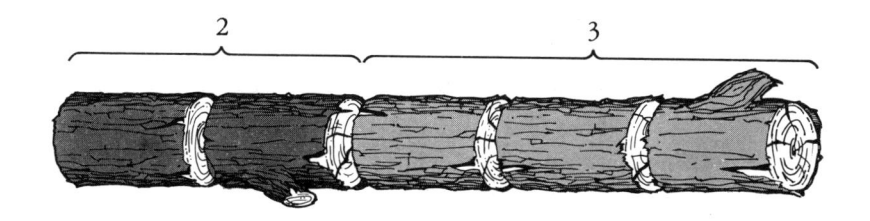

A. RATIO

1. Divide 36 cm in the ratio 4 : 5.

   Divide 36 cm into (4 + 5), i.e. 9 parts.

   $$1 \text{ part} = \frac{36}{9} \text{ cm} = 4 \text{ cm}$$

   $\therefore$ 4 parts = 4 × 4 cm = 16 cm
   and 5 parts = 5 × 4 cm = 20 cm.

2. Divide £9 in the ratio 1 : 2.
3. Divide 45 m in the ratio 2 : 3.
4. Divide £35 in the ratio 4 : 1.
5. Divide 84p in the ratio 3 : 1.
6. Divide 56 mm in the ratio 6 : 1.
7. Divide 85p in the ratio 3 : 2.
8. Divide £72 in the ratio 5 : 4.
9. Divide 108 kg in the ratio 1 : 8.
10. Divide 40 t in the ratio 3 : 7.

11. Divide £4.73 between Anne, Bill and Chris in the ratio 2 : 3 : 6.

Divide £4.73 into (2 + 3 + 6) i.e. 11 parts.

$$1 \text{ part} = \frac{£4.73}{11} = £0.43 = 43p$$

Then Anne will receive 2 × 43p = 86p
Bill will receive 3 × 43p = 129p = £1.29
and Chris will receive 6 × 43p = 258p = £2.58

12. Divide £13.80 between A, B and C in the ratio 1 : 2 : 3.
13. Divide £4.05 between Alison, Barbara and Colin in the ratio 2 : 3 : 4.
14. Divide 143p between Janet, John and Jim in the ratio 5 : 4 : 2.
15. Divide 198 cm in the ratio 2 : 1 : 3.
16. Divide 13.2 m in the ratio 4 : 5 : 2.
17. Divide £7.92 between Eileen, Fay and Glenys in the ratio 6 : 3 : 2.
18. Divide 105 g in the ratio 2 : 4 : 1.
19. Divide 117 kg in the ratio 5 : 1 : 3.
20. Divide 740 m in the ratio 5 : 3 : 2.

B. DIRECT PROPORTION

21. If 3 tyres cost £57, how much will 7 similar tyres cost?

If 3 tyres cost £57,

then 1 tyre costs $\frac{£57}{3}$

i.e. 7 tyres cost $£\frac{57}{3} \times 7 = £133$.

22. If a car uses 7 gallons of petrol for a journey of 245 miles, how many gallons would be required for a journey of 140 miles?

23. If a car uses 8 litres of petrol for a journey of 72 km, how many litres would be required for a journey of 117 km?

24. A motorcycle will travel 72 km on 6 litres of petrol. How far would it go on 10 litres?

25. A coach will run for 132 miles on 33 litres of diesel. How far would it go on 56 litres?

26. An hotel charges £93 for a stay of 6 days. How much would they charge for 10 days at the same rate?

27. A 44-seater coach for a school trip costs £242. How much would a 56-seater coach cost if the charge for each passenger is unchanged?

28. The cost of printing a book with 160 pages is £2.88. What would be the cost of printing a book with 240 pages if the cost per page remains constant?

29. The cost per mile of running a taxi is constant. If the hire charge for a 16-mile journey is £8.40, what would be the hire charge for a 28-mile journey?

30. A coach costs a fixed sum per kilometre to run. If a journey of 160 km costs a youth club £72, how far could they go for £126?

19 AVERAGES

Find the average of the following sets of numbers:

1. 5, 6, 7, 10
2. 30, 50, 80, 120
3. 6, 6, 7, 7, 9, 10
4. 15, 11, 10, 8, 7, 3
5. 1.2, 2.7, 1.8, 1.9
6. 4.3, 8.7, 2.1, 10.9
7. 5.5, 6.5, 8.5, 9.5
8. $\frac{1}{2}$, 1, $1\frac{1}{2}$
9. $\frac{1}{4}$, $\frac{1}{2}$, $\frac{3}{4}$
10. $\frac{1}{8}$, $\frac{3}{8}$, $\frac{5}{8}$

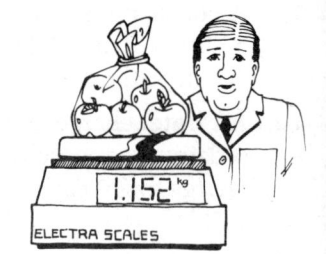

Find the average of:

11. 56p, 37p, 18p, 62p, 52p
12. £1, 50p, 24p, 66p
13. 27 g, 35 g, 14 g, 37 g, 27 g
14. 14 cm, 9 cm, 23 cm, 26 cm
15. 2 m, 5 m, 8 m, 9 m
16. 4.8 km, 1.3 km, 6.7 km, 3.2 km, 9 km
17. 1.2 litres, 3.7 litres, 0.6 litres, 3.3 litres
18. 6.2 s, 4.1 s, 9.2 s, 5.7 s
19. 16 min, 24 min, 35 min, 25 min
20. 14 °C, 18 °C, 17 °C, 20 °C, 21 °C

21. The weights of four passengers in a car are 78 kg, 70 kg, 67 kg and 73 kg. What is their average weight?

The total weight of the four passengers is:
(78 + 70 + 67 + 73) = 288 kg

$$\text{Average weight} = \frac{288}{4} \text{ kg}$$

$$= 72 \text{ kg}$$

22. The five puppies in a litter weighed 260 g, 255 g, 270 g, 265 g and 250 g. What was the average weight for the litter?

23. The 'life' of four light bulbs was 40 hours, 400 hours, 260 hours and 120 hours. What was the average life of a bulb?

24. A racing car covered the first four laps of a race in 84 s, 82 s, 85 s and 81 s. What was the average lap time?
25. Five bags of toffees contain 28, 25, 29, 32 and 26. What is the average number per bag?
26. The ages of four children in a family are 5 yrs, 10 yrs, 12 yrs and 17 yrs. Find their average age. If the mother and father are both 41 yrs, find the average age of the family.
27. The six competitors in a race took 92 s, 96 s, 100 s, 103 s, 126 s and 131 s. What was the average time for the race?
28. The weights of six eggs in a box were 71 g, 71.5 g, 69.5 g, 71 g, 72 g and 71 g. What was the average weight of an egg?
29. The number of puppies in the litters of three bitches were 2, 1 and 6. What was the average size of a litter?
30. The number of eggs found in five nests of a particular species of bird were 4, 5, 2, 5 and 2. What was the average number in a nest?
31. Use the information given on the chart below to find the average monthly rainfall for the village of Little Burton in 1984.

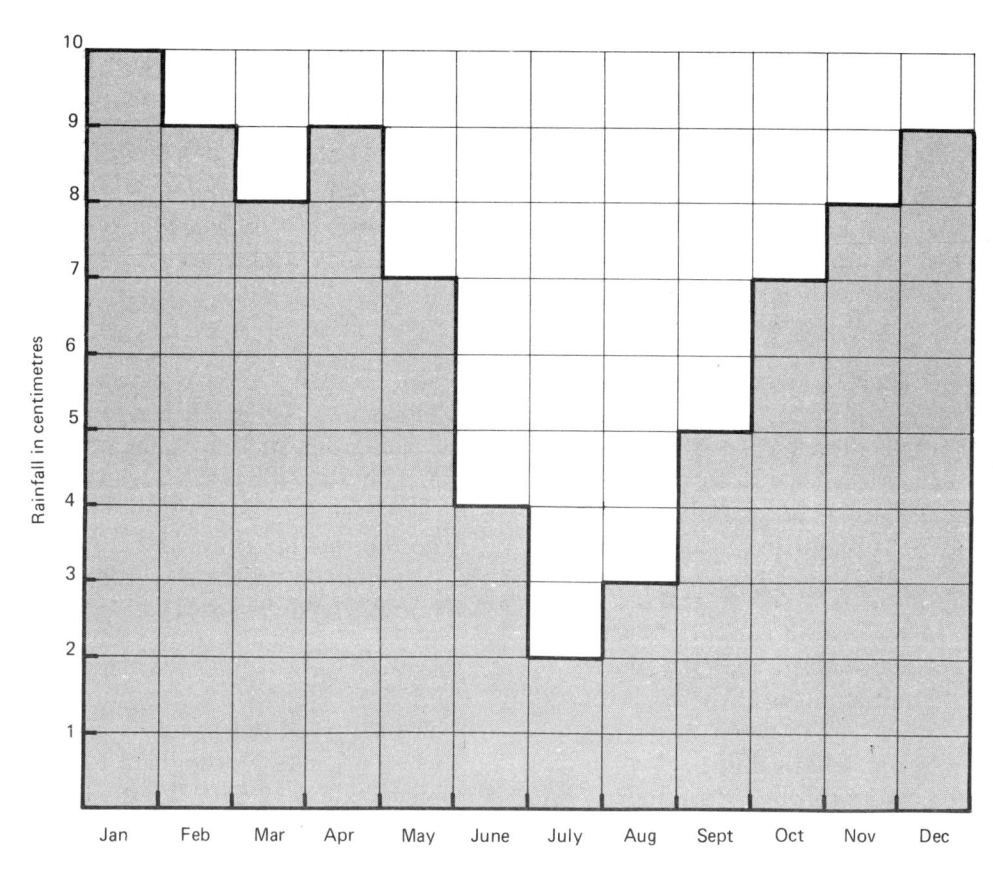

Rainfall Chart, Little Burton Village, 1984

20 DISTANCE, TIME AND SPEED

A. DISTANCE

1. Using only the routes and distances given on the map opposite, find the total distance travelled by the away team for each of the following football matches:

   (a) Southampton v Birmingham
   (b) Manchester v Sheffield
   (c) Sheffield v Newcastle
   (d) Cardiff v Stoke
   (e) Brighton v Norwich
   (f) Glasgow v Aberdeen
   (g) Liverpool v Nottingham
   (h) Birmingham v Preston
   (i) Plymouth v Ipswich
   (j) Southampton v Glasgow
   (k) Nottingham v Newcastle
   (l) Grimsby v Portsmouth
   (m) Arsenal v Newcastle
   (n) Tottenham v Liverpool
   (p) West Ham v Preston
   (q) Watford v Aberdeen
   (r) Swansea v Ipswich
   (s) Preston v Southampton
   (t) Leeds v West Ham
   (u) Grimsby v Liverpool

Questions 2–7 refer to the map opposite:

2. A coach-load of supporters leave Arsenal for an away game at Newcastle. The recorded mileage when they leave is 42 746. What will it read (a) at Leeds on the way up, (b) at Sheffield on the way back, (c) when they return to London?

3. A car-load of supporters leaves Glasgow for a match against Southampton. If the trip recorder reads 24 430 when they leave home, what will it read when they (a) pass through Birmingham on the way down, (b) pass through Manchester on the way home, (c) return to Glasgow?

4. The mileage recorder on a coach shows 64 594 when it leaves Swansea for an away game at Manchester. What will it read when the coach (a) passes through Stoke on the way up, (b) passes through Birmingham on the way home, (c) returns to Swansea?

5. The recorded mileage on a car when it leaves Nottingham for Newcastle is 12 640. What will it read (a) at Leeds on the way up, (b) at Sheffield on the way home, (c) on return to Nottingham?

Distances between various places in miles

6. A team from Cardiff travel to Sheffield. If the trip recorder reads 17 600 at Manchester on the way up, (a) what did it read at Cardiff at the beginning of the journey, (b) what will it read at Manchester on the return journey?

7. A supporters' coach travelled from Birmingham to Edinburgh via Glasgow and back again. If the recorded mileage was 38 046 at Preston on the way up, what did it read (a) at the beginning of the journey, (b) at the end of the journey, (c) at Manchester on the return trip?

8. How far will
   (a) a motorist travel in 2 hours at 50 mph?
   (b) a car travel in 3 hours at 70 km/h?
   (c) a horse travel in 5 minutes at 300 m/min?
   (d) a runner travel in 8 minutes at 5 m/s?

9. How far will
   (a) a coach travel in 1 h 30 min at 60 mph?
   (b) a lorry travel in 5 h 15 min at 80 km/h?
   (c) a ship travel in 14 hours at 12 nautical miles per hour?
   (d) an aeroplane travel in 5 hours at 330 mph?

10. How far will
    (a) an aeroplane travel in 3 h 30 min at 650 km/h?
    (b) a ship travel in 2 days at 20 nautical miles per hour?
    (c) sound travel in 4.5 s at 300 m/s?
    (d) light travel in 30 s at 3×10^8 m/s?

B. TIME

Time = Distance ÷ Speed

11. How long will
    (a) a motorist take to travel 100 miles at 50 mph?

$$\text{Time taken} = \frac{100 \text{ miles}}{50 \text{ mph}} = 2 \text{ h}$$

   (b) a lorry take to travel 300 km at 60 km/h?
   (c) a coach take to travel 175 km at 75 km/h?
   (d) a runner take to run 210 m at 6 m/s?

12. How long will it take
    (a) a ship steaming at 15 knots (nautical miles per hour) to steam 180 nautical miles?
    (b) a horse to gallop 5 km at 50 km/h?
    (c) an aeroplane to fly 2448 km at 576 km/h?

13. How long will it take
    (a) to row a boat 4 miles at 12 mph?
    (b) for a liner to cruise 5760 nautical miles at 24 knots?
    (c) a greyhound to race 204 m at 17 m/s?

C. SPEED

The diagrams below show the speedometer of a car which is in the form of a strip that moves from left to right. What speed is the car travelling at in (a) km/h, (b) mph?

14.

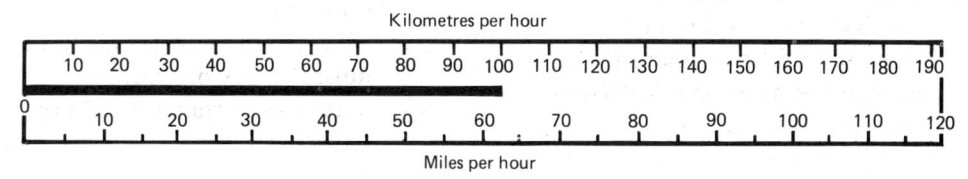

15.

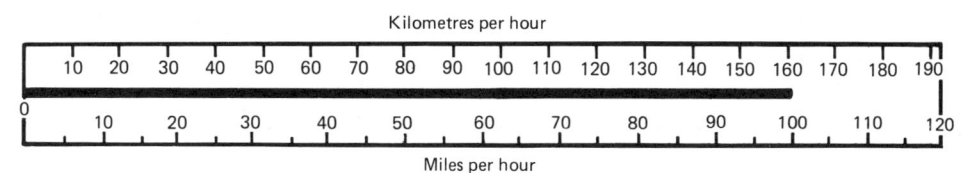

16.

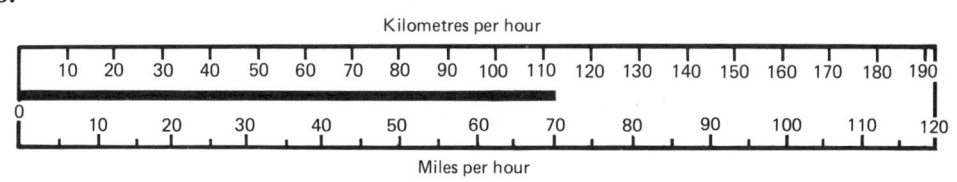

17.

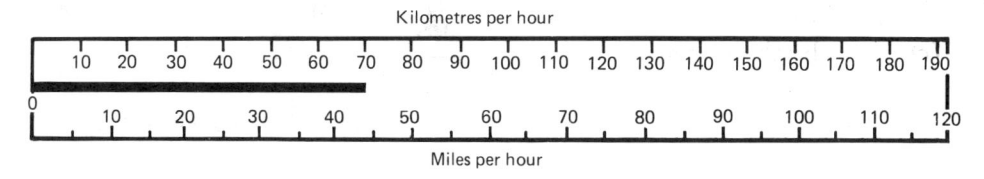

18.

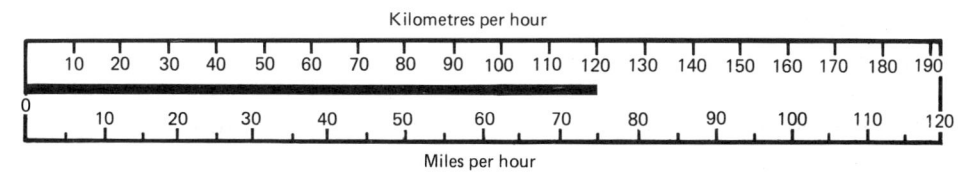

The diagrams below show the speedometer of a car. The numbers on the outside give the speed in miles per hour and the numbers on the inside show the speed in kilometres per hour. What speed is the car travelling at in (a) mph, (b) km/h?

19.

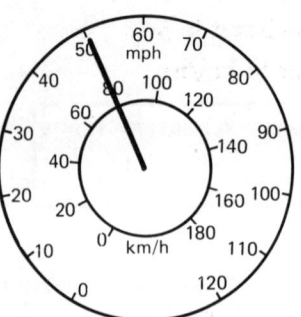

20.

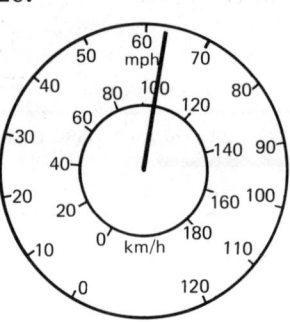

21.

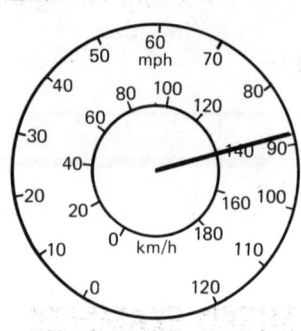

22.

23.

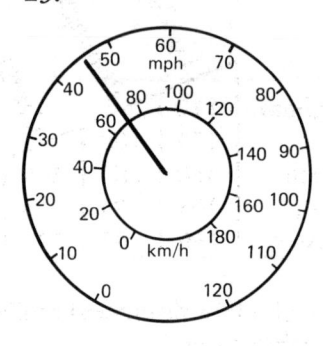

24. Find the average speed of:
(a) a woman walking 12 km in 2 hours

Average speed = Distance ÷ Time

$$= \frac{12 \text{ km}}{2 \text{ h}} = 6 \text{ km/h}$$

(b) a horse racing $1\frac{1}{2}$ miles in 3 min
(c) a car travelling 186 miles in 6 h
(d) a lorry travelling 368 km in 8 h

25. Find the average speed of:
    (a) a motorcycle travelling 165 miles in $2\frac{1}{2}$ h
    (b) a cyclist cycling 90 km in 4 h 30 min
    (c) a ship sailing 240 nautical miles in a day

26. Find the average speed of:
    (a) a cheetah running $\frac{1}{2}$ km in 20 s (answer in m/s)
    (b) an antelope running 5 km in 6 min (answer in km/h)
    (c) a racing car which laps a $3\frac{1}{2}$ km circuit in 36 s (answer in km/h)

MIXED EXAMPLES

27.

	London	Birmingham	Cardiff	Edinburgh	Liverpool
Birmingham	110				
Cardiff	155	100			
Edinburgh	380	287	365		
Liverpool	205	94	164	210	
Manchester	190	81	172	210	34

The table gives the distances in miles between six cities in the United Kingdom. Use this table to find:

(a) the distance between Cardiff and Manchester
(b) the distance between Birmingham and Liverpool
(c) the distance between London and Liverpool
(d) the time taken to go from Edinburgh to Liverpool at an average speed of 42 mph
(e) the time taken to go from Manchester to London at an average speed of 38 mph
(f) the average speed of a journey between Liverpool and Cardiff that takes 4 hours
(g) the average speed of a journey between Edinburgh and Manchester that takes $5\frac{1}{4}$ hours
(h) the average speed of a journey between Birmingham and Edinburgh that started at 1040 and finished at 1740
(i) the average speed of a journey between London and Edinburgh that started at 4.20 am and finished at 11.56 am

28.

	London	Bristol	Glasgow	Leeds	Southampton
Bristol	180				
Glasgow	635	590			
Leeds	300	330	340		
Southampton	130	120	670	380	
York	320	345	340	40	400

The table gives the distances in kilometres between six cities in the United Kingdom. Use this table to find:

(a) the distance between London and York
(b) the distance between Glasgow and Southampton
(c) the distance between Leeds and Bristol
(d) the time taken to travel from Southampton to London at an average speed of 65 km/h
(e) the time taken to travel from Leeds to Bristol at an average speed of 60 km/h
(f) the time taken to travel from Bristol to York at an average speed of 69 km/h
(g) the average speed of a journey between Glasgow and York that takes 4 hours
(h) the average speed of a journey between Bristol and Leeds that takes 6 hours 40 minutes
(i) the average speed of a journey between York and London that started at 1000 and ended at 1624
(j) the average speed of a journey between Bristol and Glasgow that started at 0732 and ended at 1920

21 TRAVEL GRAPHS

The graphs given below show six different journeys. For each journey find (a) the distance travelled, (b) the time taken, (c) the average speed.

1.

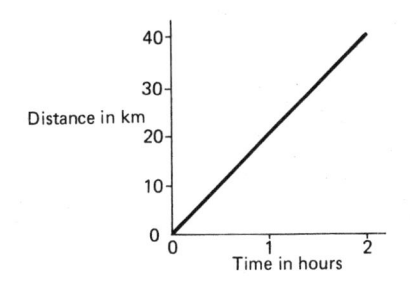

2.

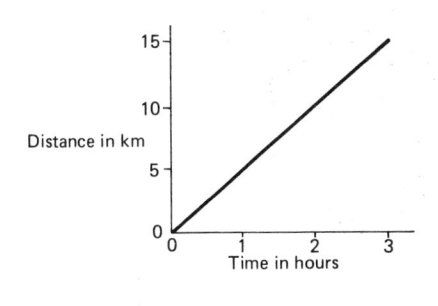

3.

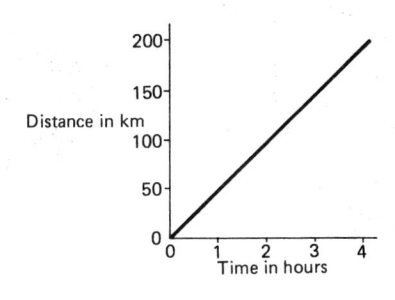

4.

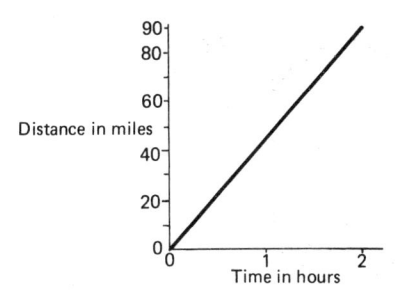

5.

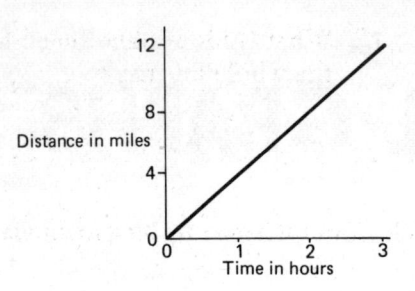

6.

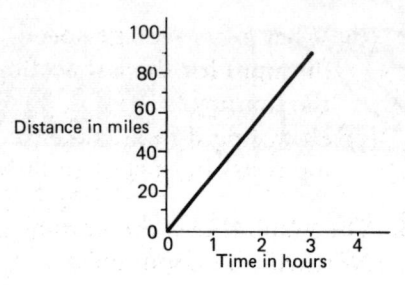

Draw travel graphs to show the following journeys:

7. 40 km in 2 h
8. 75 km in 3 h
9. 120 km in $1\frac{1}{2}$ h

10. 80 miles in 4 h
11. 125 miles in 5 h
12. 75 miles in $2\frac{1}{2}$ h

13. Sarah cycles from her home to work. The graph shows her journey.

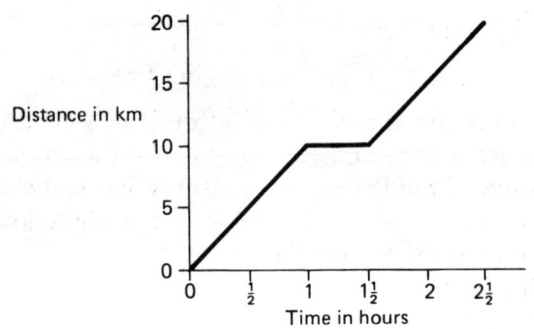

(a) How far does she cycle before she takes a rest?
(b) How long does she take before she has a rest?
(c) What is her average speed for the first part of the journey?
(d) How long does she rest?
(e) How far is it from home to work?
(f) How long does the whole journey take?
(g) What is her average speed for the whole journey?

14. John takes part in a 12-mile fun run. The graph shows his journey.

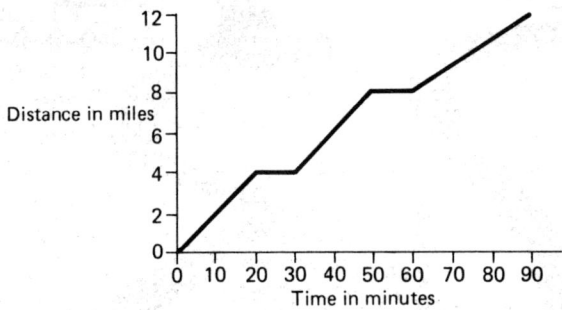

(a) How long does he spend resting?
(b) How long does he actually spend running?
(c) What is his average speed (in mph) for the first section of the journey?

(d) What is his average speed (in mph) for the last section of the journey?
(e) How long does he take (including rests) from start to finish?
(f) What is his average speed for the whole journey?

15. The graph shows the journey of a coach from Oldtown to Newtown via Northville and Southville.

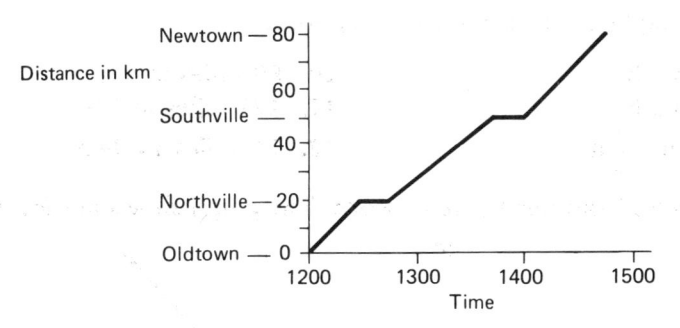

(a) How many stops are there?
(b) What is the average speed (in km/h) for each of the three stages?
(c) How far is it (i) from Northville to Southville, (ii) from Oldtown to Newtown?
(d) How long does the coach take for the whole journey?
(e) What is the average speed for the whole journey?

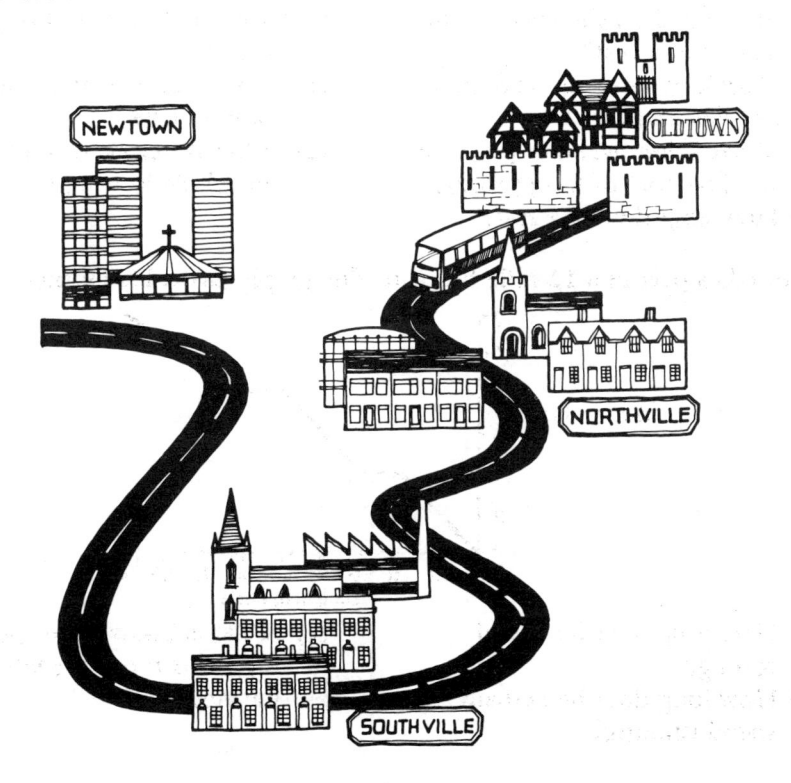

22 AREA BY COUNTING SQUARES

How many squares are required to cover each of the given areas?

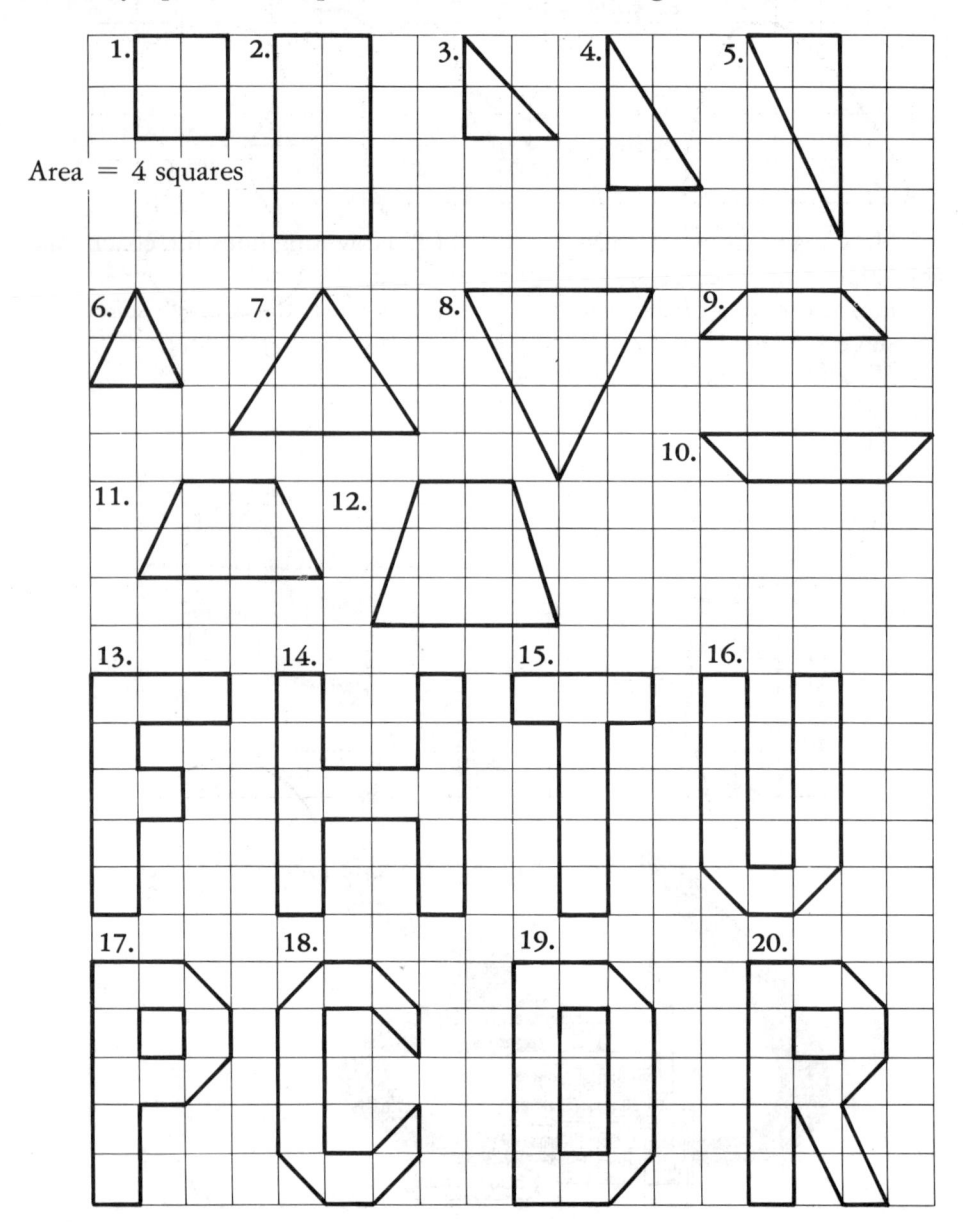

Area = 4 squares

Find the approximate area of these shapes. Count as one square those parts that are more than half a square. Ignore those parts that are less than half a square.

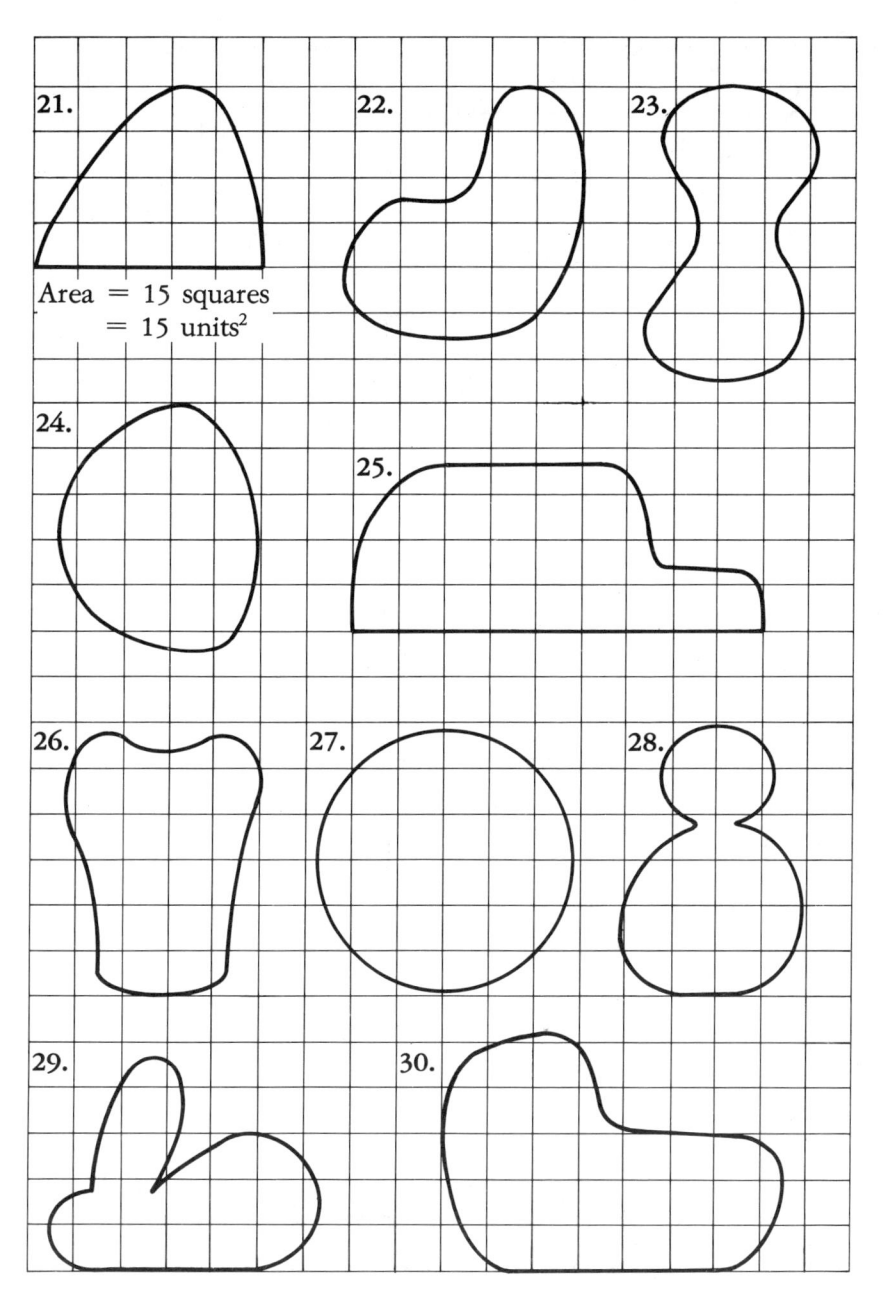

21.

Area = 15 squares
     = 15 units²

22.

23.

24.

25.

26.

27.

28.

29.

30.

31. The diagram shows the pattern for a lady's jacket. By counting squares find the area of each of the pieces A to I. Assume that each square represents a square of material of side 6 cm, i.e. has an area of 36 cm². Hence place the pieces in order according to the amount of material used (the greatest first). Use these results to find the percentage of material wasted.

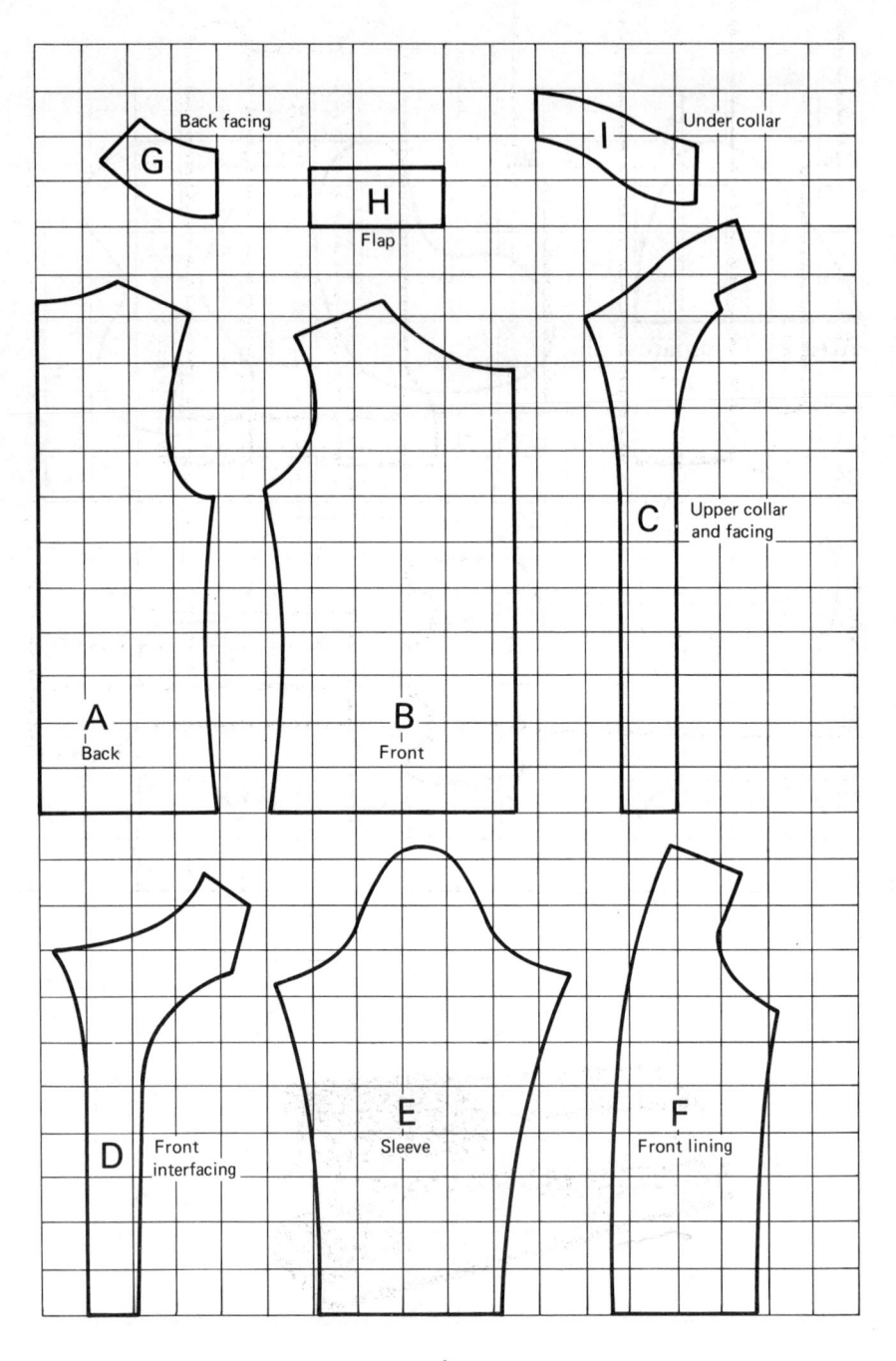

32. The diagram shows the main metal pieces for a small stapling machine. By counting squares find the area of each of the pieces A, B, C and D. Assume that each square represents one square centimetre. Hence find the percentage of metal wasted.

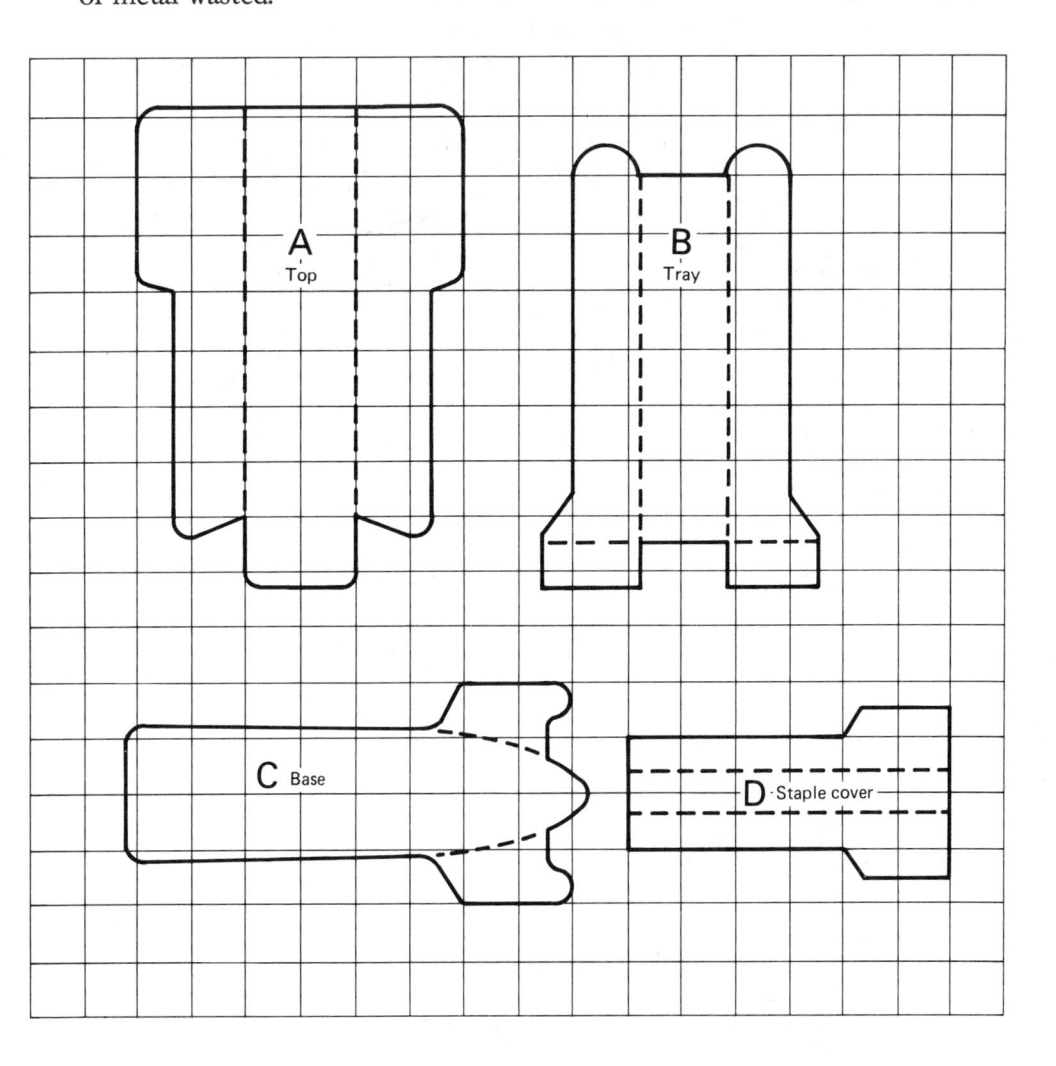

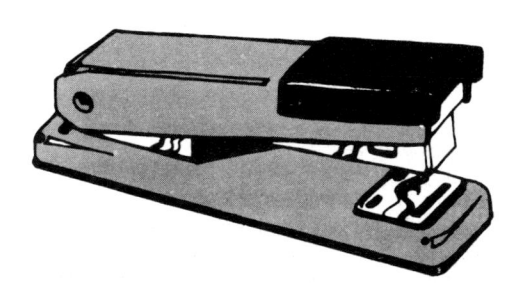

23 PERIMETER AND AREA BY CALCULATION

Find the perimeter and the area of the following shapes:

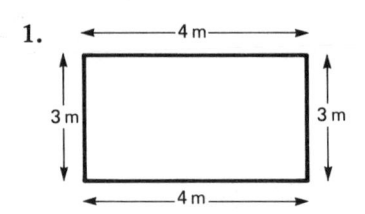

1.

Perimeter = (4 + 3 + 4 + 3) m
         = 14 m
Area = 4 × 3 m^2
     = 12 m^2

2. 6 cm, 2 cm

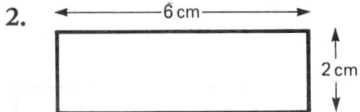

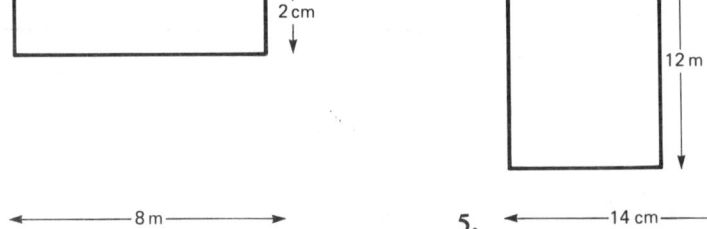

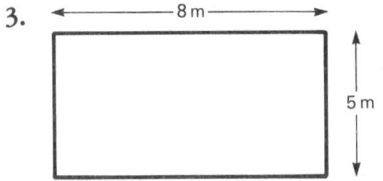

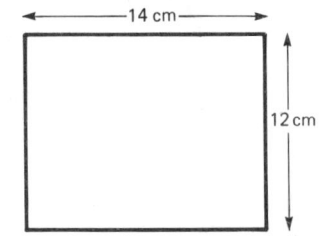

3. 8 m, 5 m

4. 8 m, 12 m

5. 14 cm, 12 cm

6.

Perimeter = (6 + 2 + 2 + 6 + 2 + 6 + 2 + 2) cm
         = 28 cm
Area = (6 × 2) + (6 × 2) cm²
     = 12 + 12 cm²
     = 24 cm²

Fill in the missing distances and then find the perimeter and area of each of the following shapes:

7.

8.

9.

10.

11.

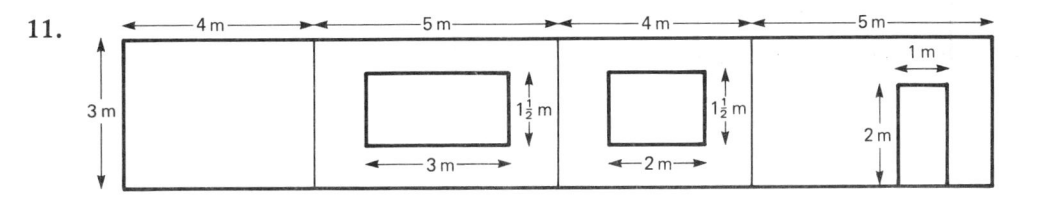

The diagram shows the four walls of my living room which has two windows and one door. Use this diagram to find:
(a) the perimeter of the room
(b) the area of the four walls *excluding* the door and windows
(c) the floor area of the room

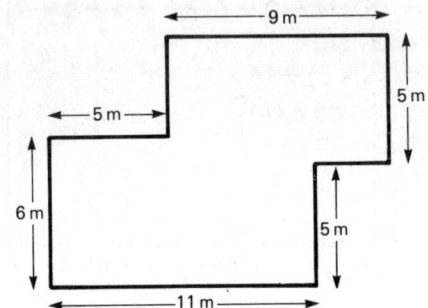

12. The diagram shows the plan of a house. Find:
    (a) the missing measurements
    (b) the perimeter of the house
    (c) its ground area

13. The diagram shows the layout of a garden, part of which has been converted into a parking area. Find the perimeter and area of:
    (a) the parking area
    (b) the lawn

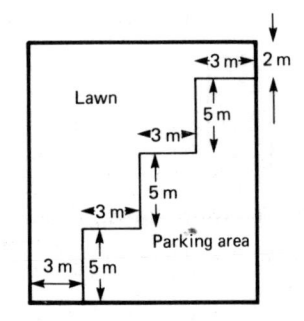

14. The diagram shows the plan of my garden. Find:
    (a) the perimeter and area of the whole plot
    (b) the perimeter and area of the vegetable plot
    (c) the area of the lawn
    (d) the area of the path

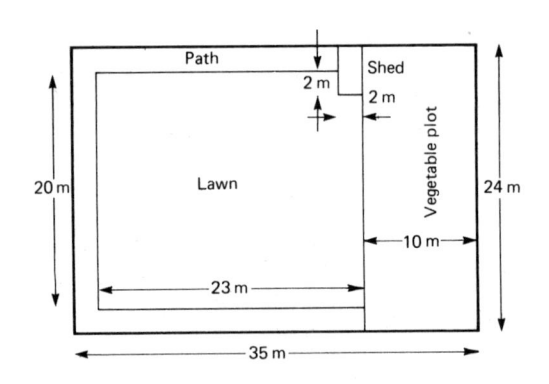

(a) Perimeter = $(35 + 24 + 35 + 24)$ m = 118 m
    Area = 35×24 m² = 840 m²
(b) Perimeter of vegetable plot = $(24 + 10 + 24 + 10)$ m = 68 m
    Area of vegetable plot = 24×10 m² = 240 m²
(c) Area of lawn = $(23 \times 20 - 2 \times 2)$ m² = $460 - 4$ m² = 456 m²
(d) Area of path = $(24 \times 2 + 23 \times 2 + 21 \times 2)$ m²
    = $(48 + 46 + 42)$ m² = 136 m²

15. The diagram shows the layout of Harold's garden. Find the perimeter and area of
    (a) the lawn
    (b) the ground occupied by flowers
    (c) the path

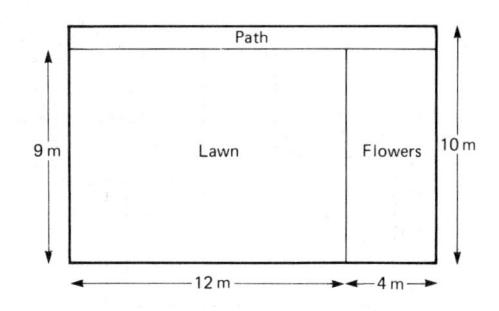

16. The diagram shows Peter's garden. If the path is everywhere 1 m wide find:
    (a) the perimeter and area of the lawn
    (b) the area of the vegetable plot
    (c) the perimeter and area of the path
    (d) the area of the flower bed

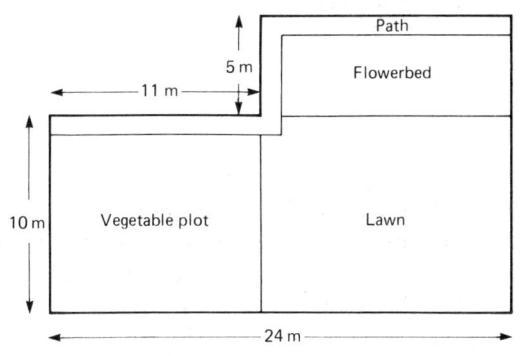

17. The diagram shows my neighbour's garden. Find:
    (a) the perimeter and area of the whole plot
    (b) the perimeter and area of the vegetable plot
    (c) the perimeter and area of the path
    (d) the area of the border
    (e) the area of the lawn

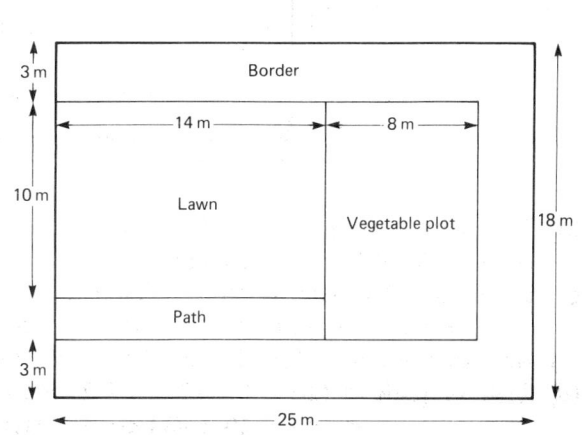

73

18.

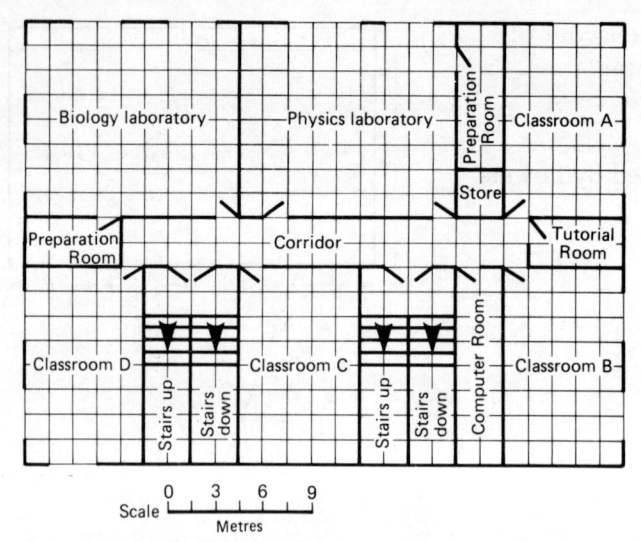

The plan shows the first-floor of a science block. Use this plan, and the scale given, to find:

(a) the length and breadth of Classroom B
(b) the length and breadth of the biology laboratory
(c) the length and breadth of the physics preparation room
(d) the length and breadth of the corridor
(e) the length and breadth of the tutorial room
(f) which room has two entrances from the corridor
(g) which room has the smallest floor area
(h) which room has the greatest length of outside wall
(i) the perimeter of classroom C
(j) which classroom has the largest floor area
(k) the area of the computer room
(l) the area of Classroom A
(m) the area of the physics laboratory
(n) the area of the biology preparation room
(p) the area of Classroom D
(q) the area of the store
(r) the area of the corridor
(s) the total area of the first floor including the stairways

Find the area of the following triangles:

19.

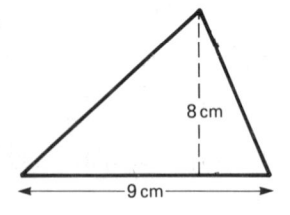

$$\text{Area} = \frac{1}{2} \text{ base} \times \text{perpendicular height}$$

$$= \frac{1}{2} \times 9 \times 8 \text{ cm}^2$$

$$= 36 \text{ cm}^2$$

74

20. (triangle, base 6 cm, height 8 cm)

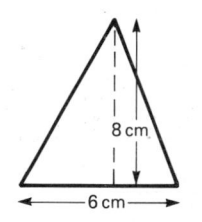

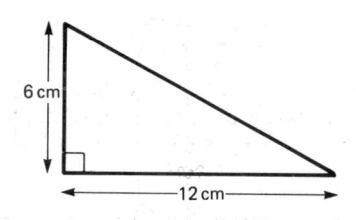

21. (triangle, base 10 cm, height 16 cm)

22. (right triangle, base 12 cm, height 6 cm)

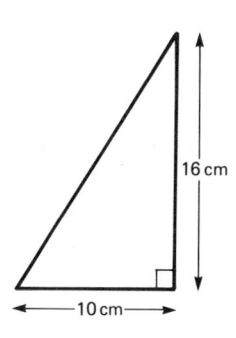

23. (triangle, base 14 cm, height 18 cm)

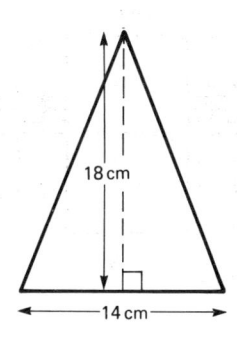

24. (triangle, base 6 cm, height 6 cm)

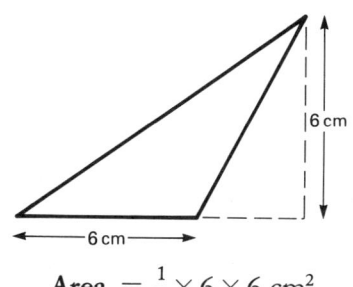

Area $= \frac{1}{2} \times 6 \times 6$ cm^2
     $= 18$ cm^2

25. (triangle, base 4 cm, height 8 cm)

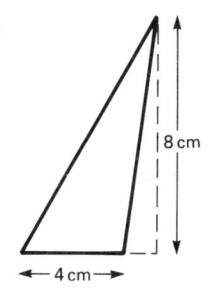

26. (triangle, base 6 cm, height 10 cm)

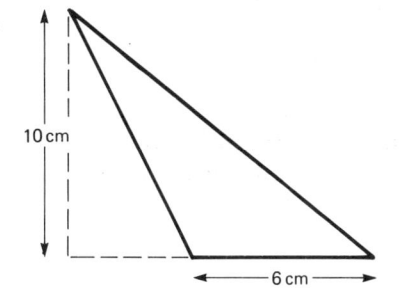

27. base 16 cm, perpendicular height 9 cm
28. base 20 cm, perpendicular height 7 cm
29. base 14 cm, perpendicular height 5 cm
30. base 13 mm, perpendicular height 18 mm
31. base 9 cm, perpendicular height 8 cm
32. base 1.8 cm, perpendicular height 0.7 cm
33. base 3.2 cm, perpendicular height 1.9 cm

Find the areas of the following figures:

34.

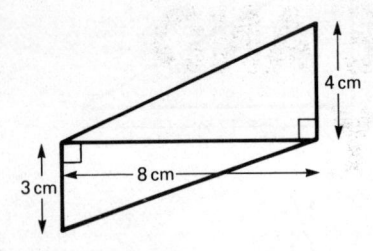

36.

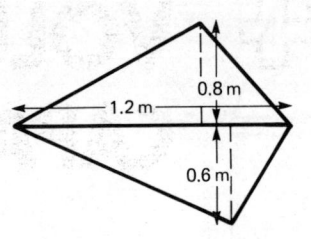

35.

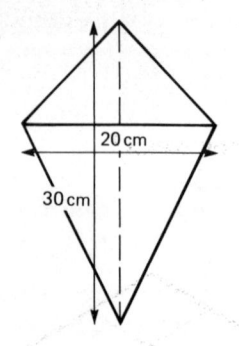

Take $\pi = \frac{22}{7}$ to find the area of a circle with:

37. Radius 7 cm:
$$\text{area of circle} = \pi r^2$$
$$= \frac{22}{7} \times 7 \times 7 \text{ cm}^2$$
$$= 154 \text{ cm}^2$$

38. radius 21 cm
39. radius 2.8 m
40. radius 49 mm
41. radius 140 m
42. diameter 14 m
43. diameter 42 cm
44. diameter 7 cm
45. diameter 0.98 m

Use your calculator and the value of π on it to find the areas of circles with the given radii/diameters. Give each answer to the first four figures on the display:

46. radius 10 cm
47. radius 3.92 m
48. diameter 32 cm
49. diameter 18.6 mm
50. radius 6.94 m

24 VOLUME AND CAPACITY

How many blocks are required to build each of the following solids?

1.

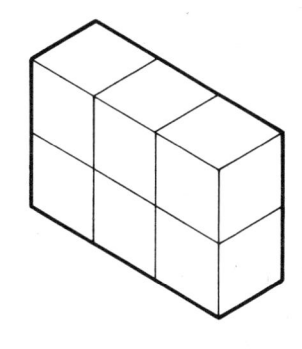

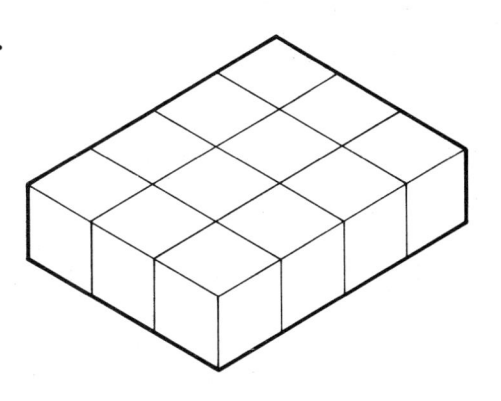

2.

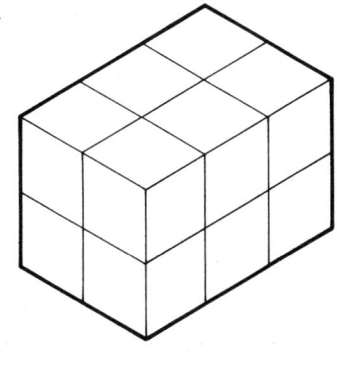

3.

4.

77

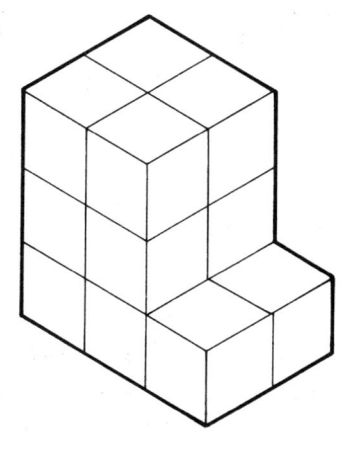

5.

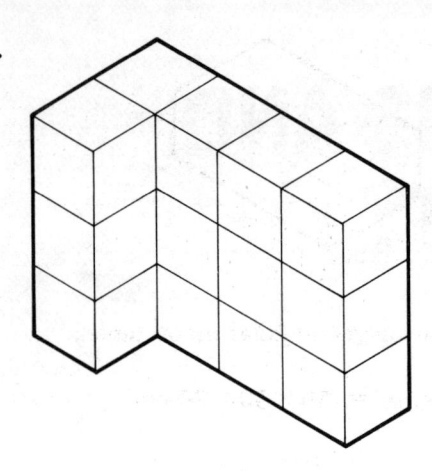

6.

Find the volume of each of the following cuboids:

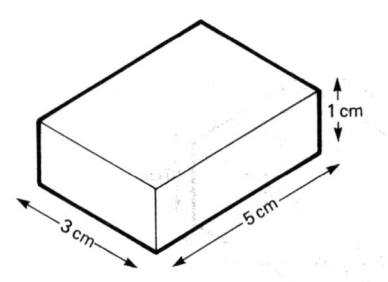

7.

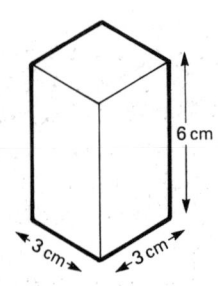

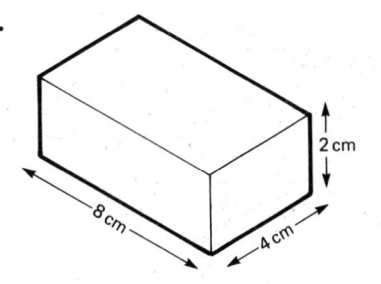

6 cm
3 cm
3 cm

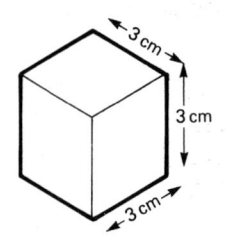

Volume = 6 × 3 × 3 cm³
= 54 cm³

10.

8 cm
2 cm
4 cm

8.

3 cm
5 cm
1 cm

11.

5 cm
5 cm
3 cm

9.

3 cm
3 cm
3 cm

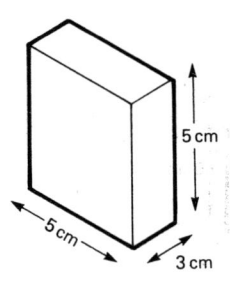

12.

$2\frac{1}{2}$ cm
4 cm
5 cm

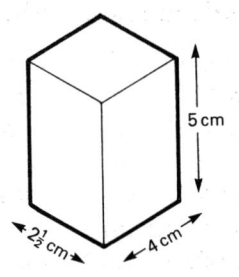

13.

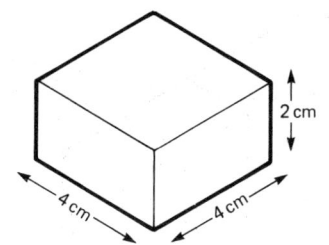

14.

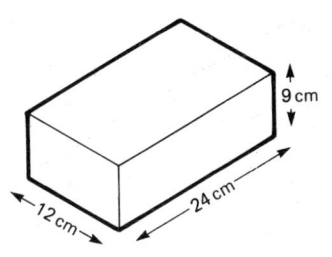

Find the capacity in litres of each of the following rectangular metal tanks:

15.

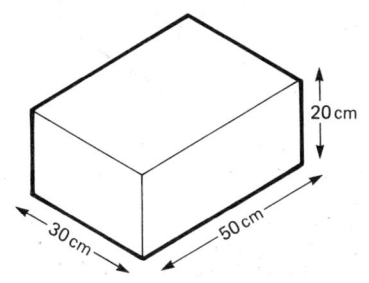

$$\text{Capacity} = 50 \times 30 \times 20 \text{ cm}^3$$
$$= 30\,000 \text{ cm}^3$$
$$= \frac{30\,000}{1000} \text{ litres}$$
$$= 30 \text{ litres}$$

16.

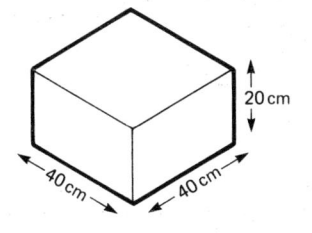

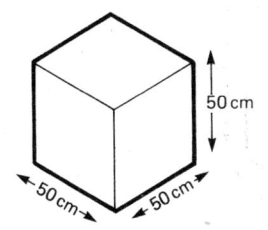

18.

17.

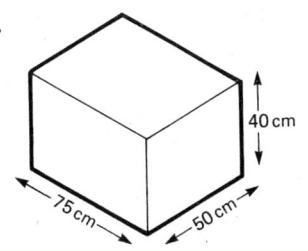

19.

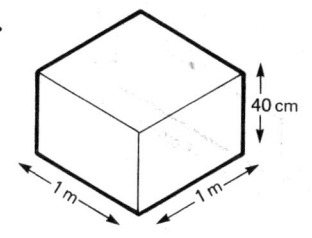

Find the volumes of the cuboids whose dimensions are as follows:

	Length	Breadth	Height
20.	3 m	2 m	1 m
21.	20 mm	10 mm	8 mm
22.	24 cm	20 cm	6 cm
23.	5 m	3 m	2 m
24.	16 cm	12 cm	7 cm
25.	35 mm	14 mm	10 mm

Use your calculator and the value of π on it to find the volumes of the given cylinders. Give your answers correct to 3 significant figures.

26.

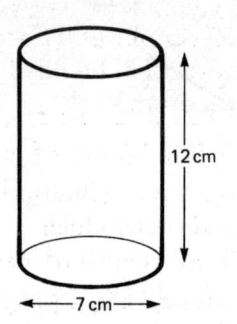

[Cylinder: 12 cm height, 7 cm diameter]

$$V = \pi r^2 h$$
$$= \pi \times \frac{7}{2} \times \frac{7}{2} \times 12 \text{ cm}^3$$
$$= 147 \pi \text{ cm}^3$$
$$= 462 \text{ cm}^3 \text{ correct to 3 sig. figs.}$$

27.

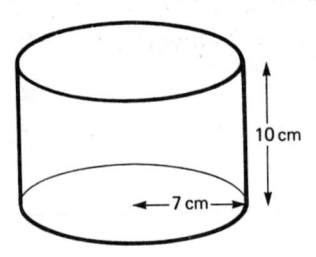

[Cylinder: 10 cm height, 7 cm diameter]

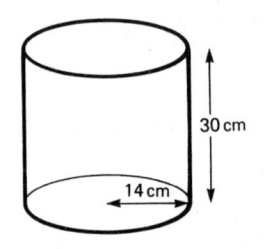

29.

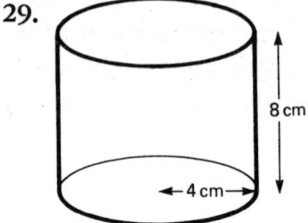

[Cylinder: 8 cm height, 4 cm diameter]

28.

[Cylinder: 30 cm height, 14 cm diameter]

30.

[Cylinder: 9 cm height, 12 cm diameter]

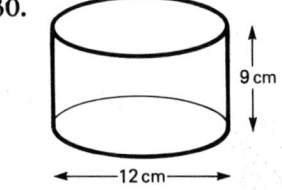

31. How many cubes of side 2 cm would fit into a rectangular cardboard box measuring 30 cm by 20 cm by 10 cm?

32. How many cubes of side 3 cm would fit into a rectangular box measuring 36 cm by 27 cm by 18 cm?

33. A rectangular stack of bricks measures 96 cm by 96 cm by 48 cm. If each brick measures 24 cm by 12 cm by 8 cm, how many bricks are there in the stack?

34. As a result of a visit to her doctor, Mrs Lewis is given a 125 ml bottle of medicine and told to take two 5 ml spoonfuls twice a day. How many complete days will the medicine last?

35. Peter Knox's doctor gives him a 250 ml bottle of medicine with instructions to take two 5 ml spoonfuls three times a day. How many complete days will it last?

36. Margaret Dent is required to take four 5 ml spoonfuls of a certain medicine three times a day for ten days. What quantity of medicine should she be given?

37. Ian Stokes is given a 500 ml bottle of medicine and told to take three 5 ml spoonfuls three times a day for eight days. How much remains in the bottle when he has completed the course?

38. A visit to the doctor for Sean Lenihan results in his being given a 350 ml bottle of medicine. If he is told to take one and a half 5 ml spoonfuls four times a day for ten days, how much will be left over?

39. Find the capacity of a cylindrical metal can of radius 4 cm and height 10 cm. Give your answer correct to the nearest 10 centilitres. How many such cans could be filled from a 20 litre drum?

40. How many $\frac{1}{2}$ litre bottles of milk may be filled from a cylindrical tank of diameter 1 m which contains milk to a depth of 50 cm?

41. Champagne glasses, when filled to just 1 cm from the top, contain 120 ml. How many glasses can be poured from a 1 litre bottle of champagne? How much is left over?

25 IMPERIAL UNITS

A. LENGTH

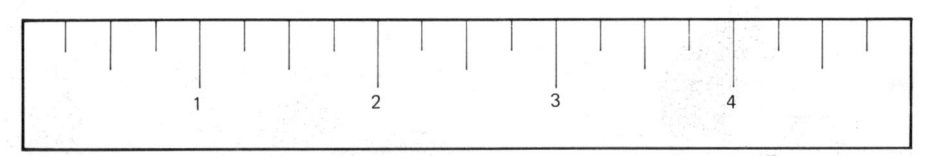

Express in inches:

1. 3 ft = 3 × 12 in = 36 in
2. 4 ft 3 in = (4 × 12 + 3) in
           = (48 + 3) in
           = 51 in

3. 2 ft
4. 5 ft
5. 10 ft
6. 40 ft
7. 12 ft 3 in
8. 4 ft 10 in
9. $3\frac{1}{4}$ ft
10. $5\frac{3}{4}$ ft

Express in feet:

11. 4 yd = 4 × 3 ft = 12 ft
12. 12 yd 2 ft = (12 × 3 + 2) ft
              = (36 + 2) ft
              = 38 ft

13. 5 yd
14. 8 yd
15. 6 yd 1 ft
16. 18 yd 2 ft
17. 22 yd
18. 440 yd

Express in feet and inches:

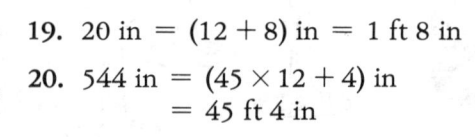

19. 20 in = (12 + 8) in = 1 ft 8 in
20. 544 in = (45 × 12 + 4) in
           = 45 ft 4 in

21. 17 in   23. 100 in   25. 316 in
22. 66 in   24. 120 in   26. 748 in

How many yards are there in:

27. 3 miles = 3 × 1760 yd = 5280 yd
28. $10\frac{1}{2}$ miles = 10.5 × 1760 yd
    = 18 480 yd

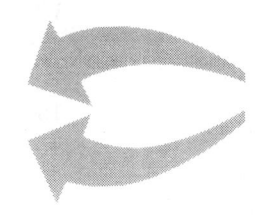

29. 26 miles   30. $4\frac{1}{4}$ miles   31. $2\frac{3}{4}$ miles   32. 12 miles

B. AREA

Find the area of rectangles with sides of the given dimensions:

	Length	Breadth	Area
1.	8 in	6 in	8 × 6 in² = 48 in²
2.	14.6 in	9.5 in	14.6 × 9.5 in² = 138.7 in²
3.	10 in	5 in	
4.	25 in	8 in	
5.	4 ft	2 ft	
6.	24 ft	9 ft	
7.	22 yd	$4\frac{1}{2}$ yd	
8.	$5\frac{1}{2}$ ft	4 ft	
9.	9 ft	2 yd	(give your answer in ft²)
10.	2 ft	8 in	(give your answer in ft²)

83

Find the area of triangles with the given dimensions:

	Length of base	Perpendicular height	Area
11.	12 in	6 in	$\frac{1}{2} \times 12 \times 6$ in² = 36 in²
12.	9 yd	7 yd	$\frac{1}{2} \times 9 \times 7$ yd² = $31\frac{1}{2}$ yd²
13.	15 in	8 in	
14.	40 in	28 in	
15.	7 in	12 in	
16.	8 ft	5 ft	
17.	20 yd	22 yd	
18.	$1\frac{1}{2}$ ft	10 in	(give your answer in in²)
19.	3 ft	30 in	(give your answer in ft²)
20.	4 ft	2 yd	(give your answer in ft²)

C. VOLUME

Find the volume of:

1. a book measuring 10 in by 8 in by 2 in

   Volume of book = 10 × 8 × 2 in³
   = 160 in³

2. a room measuring 12 ft by 10 ft by 8 ft
3. a brick measuring 9 in by $4\frac{1}{2}$ in by 3 in
4. a building block measuring 18 in by 9 in by 3 in
5. a plank of wood measuring 4 ft by 6 in by 1 in
6. a metal ingot measuring 8 in by 3 in by 2 in
7. a cube of ice of side 2 in
8. a cube of sugar of side $\frac{1}{2}$ in
9. a bale of hay measuring 3 ft by $1\frac{1}{2}$ ft by 1 ft
10. a box of cereal measuring 12 in by 9 in by 3 in

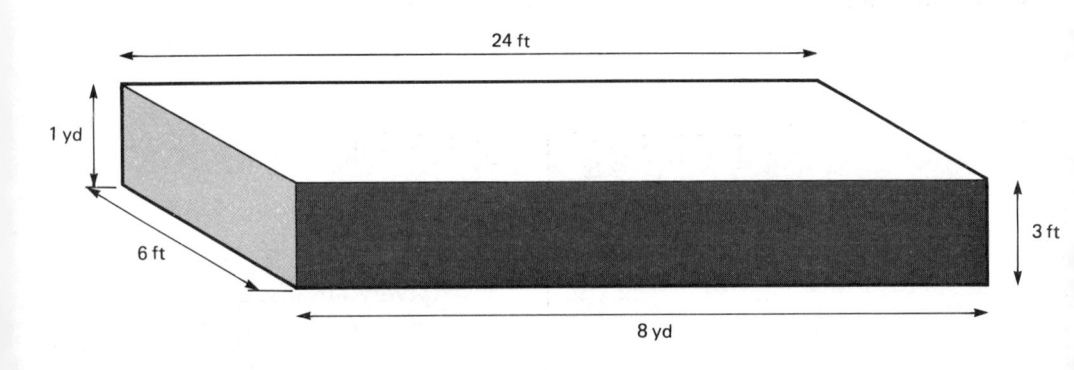

24 ft

1 yd

6 ft

3 ft

8 yd

26 METRIC AND IMPERIAL CONVERSIONS

Give your answers correct to 3 significant figures.

A. LENGTH

If 1 inch = 2.54 cm, find:

1. 2 in in cm
2. 5 in in cm
3. 12 in in cm
4. 18 in in cm
5. 20 in in cm
6. 36 in in cm

Use the same relationship, and your calculator, to find:

7. 10 cm in inches = 10 ÷ 2.54 in
   = 3.94 in correct to 3 sig. figs.

8. 15 cm in inches
9. 40 cm in inches
10. 50 cm in inches
11. 75 cm in inches

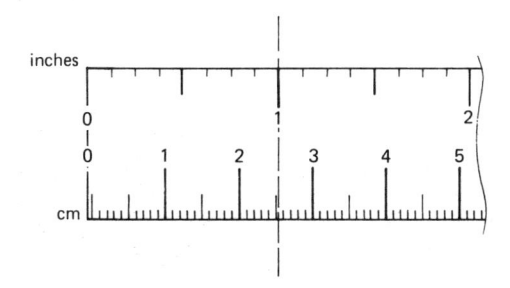

If 12 inches = 1 foot, then 1 foot = 12 × 2.54 cm = 30.48 cm
i.e. 1 foot = 30.5 cm correct to 3 sig. figs.
= 305 mm correct to 3 sig. figs.

Find:

12. 3 ft in cm = 3 × 30.48 cm
= 91.44 cm
= 91.4 cm correct to
3 sig. figs.

13. 5 ft in cm
14. 6 ft in cm
15. 8 ft in mm
16. 10 ft in mm

If 1 yard = 3 feet, then 1 yard = 91.4 cm = 914 mm = 0.914 m

Find:

17. 2 yd in mm = 2 × 914 mm
= 1830 mm correct
to 3 sig. figs.

18. 22 yd in m = 22 × 0.914 m
= 20.1 m correct to
3 sig. figs.

19. 100 m in yd = 100 ÷ 0.914 yd
= 109 yd correct to
3 sig. figs.

20. 5 yd in cm
21. 3 yd in mm
22. 80 m in yd
23. 1.4 yd in cm
24. 1500 m in yd
25. 12.6 m in yd

If 1 mile = 1760 yd = 5280 ft, then
1 mile = 1760 × 0.914 m = 1609 m to the nearest metre
= 1.61 kilometres correct to 3 sig. figs.

Find:

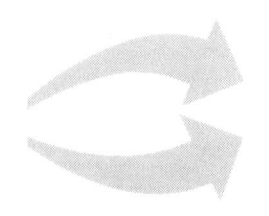

26. 5 miles in m = 5 × 1609 m
= 8050 m correct
to 3 sig. figs.

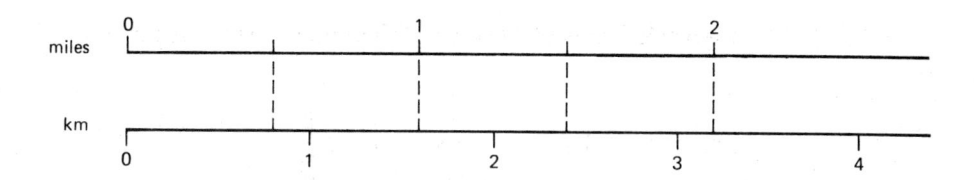

27. 3 miles in (a) m (b) km
28. 12 miles in (a) m (b) km
29. 25 miles in (a) m (b) km
30. 100 miles in km

31. 5000 m in miles = 5000 ÷ 1609 miles
    = 3.11 miles correct to 3 sig. figs.

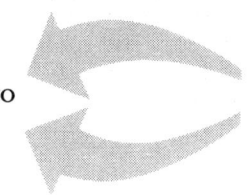

32. 12 000 m in miles
33. 15 000 m in miles
34. 10 km in miles
35. 200 km in miles

B. AREA

Since 1 in = 2.54 cm, 1 in^2 = 2.54 × 2.54 cm^2 = 6.45 cm^2 correct to 3 sig. figs.

Find:

1. 4 in^2 in cm^2 = 4 × 6.45 cm^2
   = 25.8 cm^2

2. 10 in^2 in cm^2
3. 60 in^2 in cm^2
4. 100 in^2 in cm^2
5. 144 in^2 in cm^2

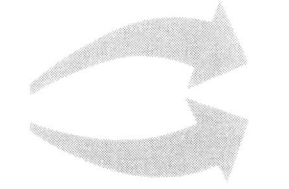

6. 10 cm^2 in in^2 = 10 ÷ 6.45 in^2
   = 1.55 in^2

7. 50 cm^2 in in^2
8. 100 cm^2 in in^2
9. 1000 cm^2 in in^2
10. 22 cm^2 in in^2

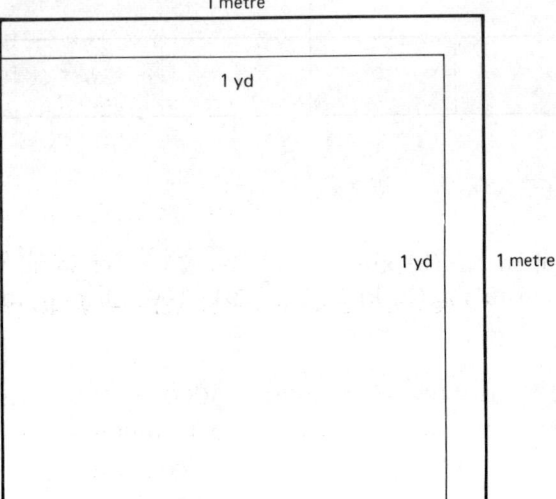

Since 1 yard = 0.914 m, 1 yd^2 = 0.914 × 0.914 m^2 = 0.8354 m^2

Find:

11. 5 yd^2 in m^2 = 5 × 0.8354 m^2
    = 4.18 m^2 correct to 3 sig. figs.

12. 3 yd^2 in m^2 13. 10 yd^2 in m^2 14. 50 yd^2 in m^2 15. 1500 yd^2 in m^2

16. 50 m^2 in yd^2 = 50 ÷ 0.8354 yd^2
    = 59.9 yd^2 correct to 3 sig. figs.

17. 20 m^2 in yd^2 18. 100 m^2 in yd^2 19. 70 m^2 in yd^2 20. 500 m^2 in yd^2

1 mile = 1.609 km ∴ 1 mile^2 = 1.609 × 1.609 km^2 = 2.589 km^2

Find:

21. 3 mile^2 in km^2 = 3 × 2.589 km^2
    = 7.77 km^2 correct to 3 sig. figs.

22. 5 mile^2 in km^2
23. 10 mile^2 in km^2
24. 25 mile^2 in km^2
25. 100 mile^2 in km^2

26. 10 km² in mile² = 10 ÷ 2.589 mile²
    = 3.86 mile² correct
    to 3 sig. figs.

27. 5 km² in mile²
28. 30 km² in mile²
29. 75 km² in mile²
30. 100 km² in mile²

1 hectare = 2.47 acres (1 acre = 4840 yd²)

Find:

31. 10 ha in acres = 10 × 2.47 acres
    = 24.7 acres

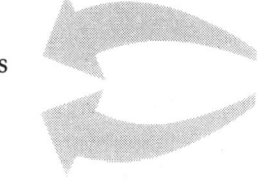

32. 5 ha in acres   33. 15 ha in acres   34. 20 ha in acres   35. 100 ha in acres

36. 50 acres in ha = 50 ÷ 2.47 ha
    = 20.2 ha correct to
    3 sig. figs.

37. 10 acres in ha
38. 30 acres in ha
39. 100 acres in ha
40. 200 acres in ha

C. VOLUME AND CAPACITY

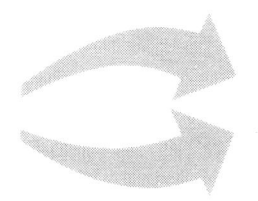

1 in³ = 16.4 cm³

Find:

1. 30 in³ in cm³ = 30 × 16.4 cm³
   = 492 cm³

2. 10 in³ in cm³   3. 25 in³ in cm³   4. 100 in³ in cm³   5. 500 in³ in cm³

6. 100 cm³ in in³ = 100 ÷ 16.4 in³
   = 6.10 in³

7. 200 cm³ in in³   8. 600 cm³ in in³   9. 1000 cm³ in in³   10. 850 cm³ in in³

1 gallon = 4.55 litres

Find:

11. 5 gallons in litres = 5 × 4.55 litres
    = 22.8 litres

12. 10 gallons in litres
13. 15 gallons in litres
14. 25 gallons in litres
15. 50 gallons in litres

16. 10 litres in gallons = 10 ÷ 4.55 gallons
    = 2.20 gallons

17. 20 litres in gallons
18. 40 litres in gallons
19. 100 litres in gallons
20. 500 litres in gallons

D. WEIGHT

1 lb = 454 g = 0.454 kg

Find:

1. 2 lb in g = 2 × 454 g = 908 g

2. 3 lb in g
3. 5 lb in g
4. 12 lb in g
5. 14 lb in g

6. 500 g in lb = 500 ÷ 454 lb
   = 1.10 lb

7. 600 g in lb
8. 800 g in lb
9. 1000 g in lb
10. 5000 g in lb

1 kg = 2.20 lb

Find:

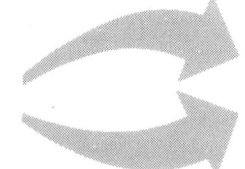

11. 5 kg in lb = 5 × 2.20 lb = 11 lb

12. 2 kg in lb
13. 8 kg in lb
14. 10 kg in lb
15. 50 kg in lb

1 metric tonne (t) = 0.984 imperial tons

Find:

16. 5 t in tons = 5 × 0.984 tons
    = 4.92 tons

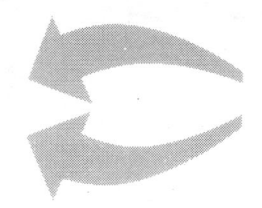

17. 3 t in tons   18. 10 t in tons   19. 15 t in tons   20. 25 t in tons

21. 3 tons in t = 3 ÷ 0.984 t
    = 3.05 t

22. 2 tons in t   23. 5 tons in t   24. 10 tons in t   25. 25 tons in t

27 VALUE ADDED TAX (VAT)

If the rate of value added tax is 15%, the price, including VAT, is found by multiplying the marked price by $\frac{115}{100}$ or 1.15. This is called the multiplying factor.

Example 1. A gold chain costs £172 + VAT at 15%.

Find the cash price.

Cash price = £172 × 1.15
= £197.80

Similarly, if the VAT rate is 18%, the multiplying factor is 1.18.

Example 2. A bicycle costs £124 + VAT at 18%.

Find the cash price.

Cash price = £124 × 1.18
= £146.32

Find the multiplying factor if the rate of VAT is:

1. 8%
2. 20%
3. 14%
4. 16%
5. 25%
6. 9%
7. 18%
8. 30%

Use your calculator, together with the correct multiplying factor, to find the cash price of the following. (Any answers that are not exact should be given correct to the nearest penny.)

9. a record marked £4.20 + VAT at 15%
10. a football marked £25 + VAT at 15%
11. a case costing £46 + VAT at 15%
12. a handbag marked £8 + VAT at 15%
13. a standard lamp marked £54 + VAT at 15%
14. a meal costing £4.40 + VAT at 18%
15. a service for the car costing £44 + VAT at 20%
16. petrol costing £10.40 + VAT at 8%
17. a fountain pen marked £4.70 + VAT at 10%
18. a typewriter marked £104 + VAT at 16%
19. a cut glass vase marked £34 + VAT at 12%
20. a bag of sweets costing £1.48 + VAT at 15%

If an article costs £27.60 including VAT at 15%, the price excluding VAT, i.e. the price before VAT was added, is found by dividing by 1.15

$$\text{i.e. price excluding VAT} = \frac{£27.60}{1.15} = £24$$

Find the price before VAT was added of:

21. a table whose cash price is £69 including VAT at 15%
22. a vase whose cash price is £9.20 including VAT at 15%
23. a lampshade whose cash price is £17.25 including VAT at 15%
24. a chair whose cash price is £287.50 including VAT at 15%
25. a radio whose cash price is £48 including VAT at 20%
26. a foodmixer whose cash price is £100 including VAT at 25%
27. a bicycle whose cash price is £125 including VAT at 25%
28. a typewriter whose cash price is £188.80 including VAT at 18%
29. a video recorder whose cash price is £336 including VAT at 12%
30. a hair dryer whose cash price is £27 including VAT at $12\frac{1}{2}$%

28 BILLS

A. ELECTRICITY BILLS

Complete the table which shows the meter readings in a block of flats at the beginning and end of a quarter:

	Flat number	Meter reading Previous	Present	Number of units used
1.	21	007231	008104	8104 − 7231 = 873
2.	22	004173	004946	
3.	23	005264	005876	
4.	24	007864	008492	
5.	25	003433	003627	
6.	26	012464	013172	
7.	27	015372	016047	
8.	28	008267	010055	

FLAT A

FLAT B

FLAT C

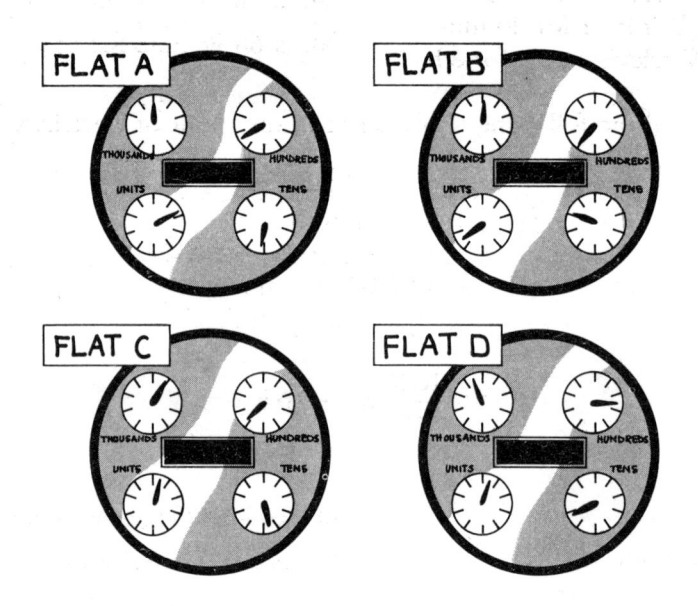

FLAT D

Calculate the quarterly electricity bills given the following information:

	Number of units used	Standing charge	Cost per unit	Total quarterly cost
9.	500	£10	5p	£10 + 500 × 5p = £10 + £25 = £35
10.	400	£12	5p	
11.	300	£15	6p	
12.	700	£14	10p	
13.	650	£10	12p	
14.	420	£9.50	8p	
15.	870	£13.50	9p	
16.	436	£10.40	7p	£10.40 + 436 × 7p = £10.40 + £30.52 = £40.92
17.	772	£8.50	5.6p	
18.	858	£14.44	4.9p	
19.	924	£15.60	8.3p	
20.	1206	£18.84	14.2p	

If one unit of electricity costs 6p, find the cost of running the following appliances for the times indicated [a unit of electricity is a kilo watt hour (kWh) which is the amount of electricity used in 1 hour by an appliance with a power rating of one kilo watt]:

21. a 3 kW electric fire for 8 h.
    Electricity used is 3 × 8 kWh i.e. 24 units. Cost of 24 units at 6p per unit = 24 × 6p = £1.44
22. a 2 kW electric fire for 5 h
23. a 1 kW hairdryer for 20 min
24. a 250 W television set for 8 h
25. a 7 kW immersion heater for 15 min
26. a 150 W refrigerator for 24 h
27. a 100 W bulb for 12 h
28. a 2 kW dishwasher for 45 min
29. an 8 kW cooker for $1\frac{1}{2}$ h
30. a 60 W bulb for 15 h

How long could the following appliances run on 1 unit of electricity?

31. a 100 W bulb.
    1 unit of electricity is 1 kWh
    i.e. 1000 W for 1 hour
    ∴ 100 W will run for
    $1 \times \frac{1000}{100}$ h i.e. 10 h

32. a $2\frac{1}{2}$ kW electric fire
33. a 250 W bulb
34. an 8 kW shower heater
35. a 200 W television set

B. GAS BILLS

Calculate the gas bills for each of the following householders who pay their bill using the Credit Tariff:

	Name	Number of therms used	Standing charge	Cost of gas per therm	Total quarterly charge
1.	Miss Deats	400	£8	30p	£8 + 400 × 30p = £8 + 12 000 p = £8 + £120 = £128
2.	Mr Hanks	500	£10	40p	
3.	Miss Jenner	800	£9	30p	
4.	Mr Korol	600	£15	45p	
5.	Mrs Midgley	700	£20	35p	
6.	Miss Porter	1000	£18	38p	
7.	Mr Short	450	£16	42p	
8.	Mrs Sturdy	950	£14.50	38p	
9.	Mrs Hanes	826	£16.75	50p	
10.	Mr Kumar	444	£20.40	55p	

Calculate the quarterly gas bills for each of the following householders who pay for their gas using the Domestic Prepayment Tariff:

	Name	Number of therms used	Standing charge	Price per therm for first 50 therms	Price per therm for further therms	Total quarterly charge
11.	Mr Tamlin	300	£5	60p	30p	£5 + 50 × 60p + 250 × 30p = £5 + £30 + £75 = £110
12.	Mrs Yates	400	£5	50p	30p	
13.	Miss Lewis	500	£8	40p	20p	
14.	Miss Toms	600	£10	60p	30p	
15.	Mr Virgo	450	£9	55p	30p	
16.	Mr Powell	350	£12	45p	25p	
17.	Mrs Thomas	270	£8.50	65p	35p	
18.	Mr White	520	£7.70	67p	38p	
19.	Mr Ward	426	£9.30	54p	32p	
20.	Mrs Wynn	732	£12.80	72p	54p	

C. TELEPHONE BILLS

Calculate the quarterly telephone bills for the following households:

	Household	Quarterly rental	Units used	Cost per unit	Total, exclusive of VAT
1.	Miles	£15	600	6p	£15 + 600 × 6p = £15 + £36 = £51
2.	Thomas	£13.50	700	6p	
3.	Smith	£14	400	5p	
4.	Jenkins	£16	750	8p	
5.	Hutton	£18.40	650	5.5p	
6.	Carney	£20	480	7.4p	
7.	Wilcox	£15.50	518	8.4p	
8.	Tucker	£13.70	413	10p	
9.	Street	£18.70	834	11p	
10.	McGeorge	£21	912	12p	

11. (a) Total payable = £51 × 1.15
    = £58.65
    (b) Total payable = £51 × 1.23
    = £62.73

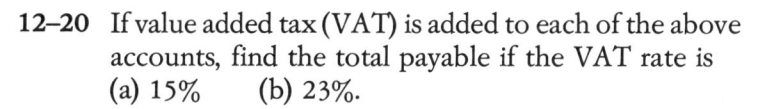

12–20 If value added tax (VAT) is added to each of the above accounts, find the total payable if the VAT rate is
(a) 15%   (b) 23%.

29 INSURANCE

A. HOUSE INSURANCE

Find the yearly cost of insuring the following houses if the premium is £1.50 per £1000 insured:

	Value of house	Premium required
1.	£40 000	£1.50 × 40 = £60
2.	£55 000	£1.50 × 55 = £82.50
3.	£20 000	
4.	£30 000	
5.	£35 000	
6.	£45 000	
7.	£60 000	
8.	£72 000	
9.	£36 000	
10.	£126 000	

B. INSURANCE OF HOUSE CONTENTS

Find the yearly cost of insuring the contents of a house if the premium is 35p per £100 insured:

	Value of contents	Total premium required
11.	£5000	35p × 50 = £17.50
12.	£9500	35p × 95 = £33.25
13.	£10 000	
14.	£8000	
15.	£14 000	
16.	£30 000	
17.	£7500	
18.	£12 500	
19.	£22 500	
20.	£18 500	

C. INSURANCE OF ARTICLES UNDER 'ALL RISKS'

Find the yearly cost of insuring articles to the given value under the 'all risks' section of a policy if the rate is 1p in the £:

	Value of article(s)	Total premium required
21.	£200	200 × 1p = £2
22.	£560	560 × 1p = £5.60
23.	£700	
24.	£1200	
25.	£2400	
26.	£5700	
27.	£12 600	
28.	£440	
29.	£860	
30.	£954	

D. MOTOR INSURANCE

Motor Safe Insurance Company Comprehensive Insurance Cover

District	\multicolumn{5}{c}{Insurance group}
	1	2	3	4	5
A	300	400	550	700	1000
B	330	450	600	750	1100
C	350	475	650	850	1200
D	400	550	750	1000	1350
E	440	600	900	1200	1500

The above rates apply to owners over 25 years old. For drivers aged 17–25 add 50%. Use this information to find the premiums due for each of the following car owners:

31. Ford Escort 1.6GL group 4; district C; aged 50
32. Morris Marina 1300 group 2; district E; aged 43
33. Renault 18 GTL group 4; district A; aged 34
34. Ford Sierra group 3; district D; aged 21

35. Mini Metro group 2; district B; aged 23

36. Rover 2300 group 4; district A; aged 22

37. Vauxhall Carlton group 3; district B; aged 56

38. Citroen GSA Club group 3; district E; aged 60

39. Ford Fiesta 1100 group 2; district A; aged 24 with 50% no claims discount

40. Princess 1800 group 4; district E; aged 35 with 40% no claims discount

30 WAGES AND SALARIES

A. WAGES

Find the gross weekly wage:

	Name	Hours worked	Hourly rate	Gross wage
1.	Phil Sparks	40	£2	£2 × 40 = £80
2.	Herbert Zippel	38	£4	
3.	Bill Siggers	42	£3	
4.	Tim Horton	37	£4.50	
5.	Ralph Hopkins	47	£2.20	
6.	Linda Fish	50	£3.53	
7.	Richard Ellis	$36\frac{1}{2}$	£4.12	
8.	Sean Donovan	$44\frac{1}{2}$	£3.88	
9.	Jack Minet	$54\frac{1}{4}$	£2.48	

Find the hourly rate of pay:

	Name	Hours worked	Gross pay	Hourly rate
10.	Fred Saleh	36	£72	$\frac{£72}{36} = £2$
11.	Vicki Marshall	41	£123	
12.	Bernard Hoare	39	£136.50	
13.	Susan Hall	54	£154.98	
14.	Mary Salter	48	£118.08	
15.	Mike Leggett	$38\frac{1}{2}$	£122.43	
16.	Lorna Davies	$46\frac{1}{2}$	£164.61	

Find the number of hours worked:

	Name	Gross wage	Hourly rate	Number of hours worked
17.	Rita Salisbury	£120	£3	$\frac{120}{3}$ h = 40 h
18.	Jean Hopwood	£72	£2	
19.	Peter Pring	£124.80	£2.60	
20.	Alan Rogers	£92.22	£1.74	
21.	Douglas Jenkins	£109.98	£2.82	
22.	Tino Salvatore	£131.14	£3.16	

Find the net pay:

	Name	Gross pay	Deductions	Net pay
23.	Beryl Black	£94.60	£21.25	£94.60 − £21.25 = £73.35
24.	Sally Green	£104.20	£30.15	
25.	Norman Gifford	£162.15	£42.40	
26.	Peter Thomas	£121.84	£34.50	
27.	Sean Duggan	£182.94	£47.21	
28.	Audrey Manson	£204.50	£62.76	

Find the net pay:

	Name	Gross pay	National insurance	Income tax	Net pay
29.	Colin Giles	£94.50	£7.44	£20.14	£94.50 − £7.44 − £20.14 = £66.92
30.	Eileen Vincent	£122	£8.66	£28.53	
31.	John Lewis	£114.50	£8.04	£30.40	
32.	Peter Smith	£162.80	£12.16	£32.89	
33.	Alma Higgins	£174.74	£14.44	£58.27	
34.	Penny Yates	£216.50	£16.73	£62.70	

Find the net pay per hour for overtime:

	Name	Basic hourly rate	Overtime rate	Overtime pay for each hour worked
35.	Tom Owen	£3	time and a half	£3 × $1\frac{1}{2}$ = £4.50
36.	Richard March	£2.50	time and a half	
37.	Phil Roche	£1.84	time and a half	
38.	Sue Elliott	£3.17	double time	
39.	Anne King	£4.40	time and a quarter	
40.	John Brakworth	£5.64	time and a half	

B. SALARIES

Find the annual (yearly) salary of these people:

1. A bank manager with a salary of £1500 per calendar month

   Yearly salary = £1500 × 12
   = £18 000

2. Dr Peter Brown with a salary of £2000 per calendar month
3. Jenny May with a salary of £1000 per calendar month
4. George Staley with a salary of £1200 per calendar month
5. Edith Berne with a salary of £800 per calendar month
6. John Lyddon with a salary of £950 per calendar month
7. Helen Shortman with a salary of £1450 per calendar month
8. Elsie Perry with a salary of £1100 per calendar month
9. Hugh Francis with a salary of £1324 per calendar month
10. Robert Wayne with a salary of £1675 per calendar month

Newspapers frequently advertise jobs giving the pay as a yearly salary. Find the pay each calendar month for:

11. Ken Wood who earns £15 600 each year

    Pay each calendar month

    $= \dfrac{£15\ 600}{12} = £1300$

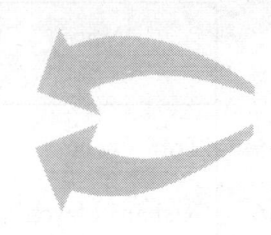

12. Jack Burton who earns £12 000 each year
13. Edna Ellis who earns £9600 each year
14. Tom Kinear who earns £14 400 each year
15. Gladys Bell who earns £19 200 each year
16. Mary Smith who earns £24 000 each year
17. Doris Posnett who earns £10 320 each year
18. Peter Barker who earns £13 680 each year
19. Alison Leeson who earns £18 864 each year
20. Peggy Norman who earns £22 164 each year

31 BUDGETING, OR 'WHERE THE MONEY GOES'

All income in this exercise is considered to be net, i.e. take-home pay.

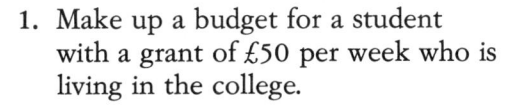

1. Make up a budget for a student with a grant of £50 per week who is living in the college.

Board and lodging	£20
Fares	£8
Lunches	£5
Clothes	£4
Pleasure	£8
Books and stationery	£5

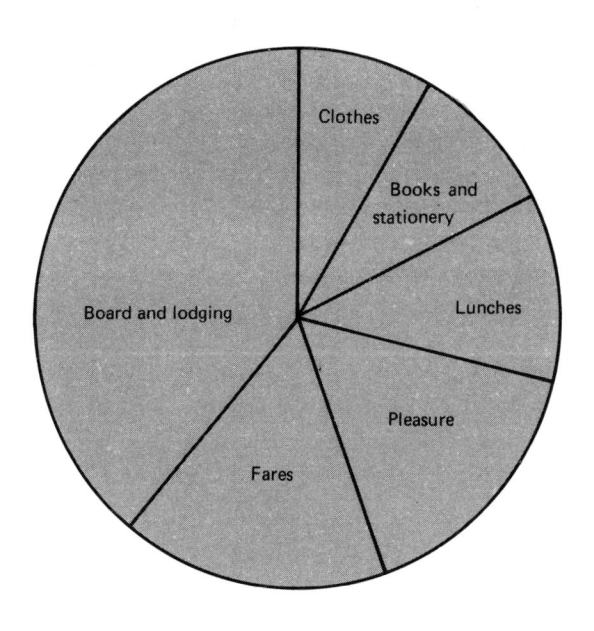

Make up a possible budget for:

2. a housewife with two children who receives £100 per week from her husband
3. a secretary earning £80 per week who lives in a flat on her own and pays rent for it
4. a student receiving £50 who rents a flat with four other students
5. a schoolteacher earning £180 per week who owns his own house and is married with one child
6. a £120 per week bachelor who is buying his own house
7. a single man living at home with his parents who earns £160 per week but is a heavy smoker
8. a single lady living with her parents who earns £140 per week and hopes to get married next year

32 BANKS AND BUILDING SOCIETIES

A. BANKING: PAYING IN

Counterfoil (kept by customer):

Date	8/2/85	
Credit	P. K. Ellis	
£20 Notes	40	
£10 Notes	50	
£5 Notes	75	
S. & I. Notes		
£1	18	
50p	7	50
Silver	6	40
Bronze	1	54
Total Cash	198	44
Cheques, P.O.'s etc. see over	54	12
£	252	56

Paying in slip (kept by bank):

bank giro credit

Date 8/2/85
Cashier's stamp & initials
Code No. 40-12-15
Bank **Northland Bank plc**
Branch **Blackwood**

Credit P. K. Ellis
Account No. 40342617

SF 819 Fee No. of Cheques Paid in by R. Stanley Ref. No.

£20 Notes	40	
£10 Notes	50	
£5 Notes	75	
S. & I. Notes		
£1	18	
50p	7	50
Silver	6	40
Bronze	1	54
Total Cash	198	44
Cheques, P.O.'s etc. see over	54	12
£	252	56

1. Use the paying-in slip to answer the following questions:
   (a) How much was paid in 'in notes'?
   (b) How much was paid in 'in coin'?
   (c) How many £5 notes did Mr Ellis pay in
   (d) What was the total value of the cash?
   (e) What was the total value of cheques and postal orders?
   (f) How many 50p coins were paid in?

2. Copy the paying-in slip given in question 1 and enter the following information on it. Use today's date and your own name:
   three £20 notes, five £5 notes, sixteen 50p pieces, £4.25 in silver and £3.16 in bronze

In the following questions make a copy of the counterfoil:

3. fourteen £5 notes, nine 50p pieces, £7.40 in silver

4. eight £10 notes, twenty-six £5 notes, £32.65 in silver, £2.16 in bronze

107

5. thirteen £10 notes, thirty-three £5 notes, £17.30 in silver, £4.44 in bronze
6. six £20 notes, £48.75 in silver and £8.62 in bronze
7. two £20 notes, one hundred and five £5 notes, £62 in silver
8. five £10 notes, seventy-three £5 notes, thirty-seven 50p pieces and £23.80 in silver
9. thirty-four £20 notes, twenty-one £10 notes and sixty-four £5 notes
10. forty-six £5 notes, twenty-three 50p coins, £72.60 in silver, £24.93 in bronze

B. BANK STATEMENTS

Northland Bank plc
91 High Street
Cardport
Sussex

E. L. STEVENS ESQ.

Statement of Account

1984	Sheet 47	Account No 24753446	Debit	Credit	Balance Credit C	Debit D
April 6	Balance brought forward				342.66 C	
April 13	569147		63.44		279.22 C	
April 13	569150		17.12		262.10 C	
April 13	569149		18.20		243.90 C	
April 13	569148		10.00		233.90 C	
April 27	569151		2.38		241.52 C	
April 30	Grangeway Payments A/C			526.55	768.07 C	
May 4	E. L. STEVENS B A/C		210.00		558.07 C	
May 8	569152		142.65		415.42 C	
May 8	569153		15.18		400.24 C	
May 10	569155		29.13		371.11 C	
May 11	569156		9.43		361.68 C	
May 14	569154		3.75		357.93 C	
May 17	569157		24.13		333.80 C	
May 24	569159		16.08		317.72 C	
May 25	569158		419.14			101.42 D
May 29	569160		18.24			119.66 D
May 31	Grangeway Payments A/C			519.70	400.04 C	
June 1	E. L. STEVENS B A/C		210.00		190.04 C	
June 4	569161		40.00		150.04 C	
June 4	569163		15.80		134.24 C	
June 4	569162		19.07		115.17 C	
June 4	569164		5.67		109.50 C	
June 7	569165		29.83		79.67 C	
June 11	CHARGES		5.13		74.54 C	
June 13	SUNDRIES			307.42	381.96 C	
June 13	569166		154.72		227.24 C	

Use the previous statement (p. 108) to answer the following questions:

1. What was the balance in the account on (a) April 27, (b) May 10, (c) June 6?
2. On which day(s) was there (a) most in the account, (b) least in the account?
3. How much did the bank deduct for bank charges?
4. What was the value of the cheques paid out of the account on (a) April 13, (b) June 4?
5. What do you think Mr Stevens earned, after deductions, in a year? Give your answer correct to the nearest £1000.
6. Why do you think the cheque numbers do not appear on the statement in numerical order even though the cheques were probably written in numerical order?
7. How much does Mr Stevens pay into his B account (a) each month, (b) in a year?
8. What was the largest cheque Mr Stevens wrote? On which day was it paid from his account?
9. What was the smallest cheque Mr Stevens wrote? On which day was it paid from his account?
10. How much was paid into the account during the period of the statement?
11. When the next statement arrives (a) what sheet number will it show, (b) what will be the balance brought forward?
12. How many days was the account overdrawn?
13. When do you think Mr Stevens receives his pay?
14. How much was paid out of the account during the month of May?
15. How much was paid out of the account between 13 May and 12 June?

C. BUILDING SOCIETY ACCOUNTS

A page from John Smith's Investment Account with the Liverpool Permanent Building Society is on the next page. Use it to answer the following questions:

1. What was the greatest amount in the account during the period?
2. How much was in the account on (a) 14 September, (b) 10 October, (c) 1 February?
3. What was the largest amount withdrawn on any one day?
4. What was the total put into the account during the period?
5. What was the total withdrawn from the account during the period?
6. How much *cash* was paid into the account between 20 August and 1 March?
7. How much did Mr Smith receive in interest from the building society?
8. How often do you think 'interest' is paid?
9. What was the total value of the cheques drawn on the account?
10. What advantage does this page suggest that the building society account has over the bank account given earlier? Can you think of any others?

109

NAME: MR. JOHN SMITH

Roll Number: 3R 4264901

Date	Cashier's initials	Description	Withdrawn		Invested		Balance	
15 8 84	ED	Balance brought forward					324	13
15 8 84	ED	Cash	60	00			264	13
14 9 84	BA	Chq.	108	44			155	69
30 9 84	Interest				12	16	167	85
16 10 84	BA	Cash	40	00			127	85
30 10 84	JB	Cash			25	00	152	85
13 11 84	ED	Chq.	52	82			100	03
13 11 84	ED	Chq.			126	14	226	17
30 11 84	ED	Cash			214	00	440	17
4 12 84	BA	Cash	100	00			340	17
10 12 84	BA	Cash	125	00			215	17
18 1 85	JB	Cash			35	00	250	17
31 1 85	ED	Cash	150	00			100	17
2 2 85	BA	Cash	20	00			80	17
5 3 85	JB	Cash	45	00			35	17
31 3 85	Interest				18	68	53	85
4 4 85	BA	Chq.			184	37	238	22
16 4 85	BA	Cash	120	00			118	22

33 RENTAL CHARGES

HARRY'S HEAVY DUTY
TOOL HIRE Tel. 30645

Weekly Rates	£
Hoover Mower	4.50
Conventional Power Mower	5.75
Power Saw	10.95
Compact Cement Mixer	25.50
Selection of Hand Implements (spade, fork, pick, hoe, rake, etc.)	2.50
Electric Hedge Cutters	3.25
Rotivator	12.50
Mini-Tractor-Mower	37.45
Hand Saw and Work Bench	6.30
Hydraulic Jack and Ramps	16.87
Selection of Power Drills	7.50

1. A TV set is rented at £9.60 per calendar month or £108 per year. How much is saved by paying once a year?
2. The rental for a flat is £34 per week. How much is this each year?
3. The Burns family pays £26 per week rent for their house. How much is this each year?
4. A video recorder may be hired for £5 per week. How much is this each year?
5. The monthly hire charge for a music centre is £12.60. How much is this each year?
6. Esther Newton rents a flat for £1040 per year. How much is this per week?
7. A TV dealer offers to rent a colour set for £102 per year or £9.20 per calendar month. How much more does it cost if you pay each month?
8. Kevin McCarthy hires a van for 4 days at a cost of £37.60. How much extra would be charged if he kept it a further day?
9. A couple hire glasses for their wedding reception at a cost of 78p per dozen. How much will it cost to hire (a) 144, (b) 200?

10. Peter Guy hired a roof rack for his car to go on holiday. The hire charge is £1.50 plus 30p per day. How much would it cost him for a 15-day holiday?

11. Copy and complete the following table of hire charges.
Assume that an article hired for 4 weeks will cost four times as much as one hired for one week, and so on.

| | Hire or rental charge ||||
Article	per day	per week	per month (4 weeks)	per year (52 weeks)
TV set	—		£8	
Video recorder	—		£12	
Concrete mixer		£7		—
Motor car			£112	—
Waste disposal skip		£10.50		—

12. The terms for hiring a concrete mixer from *Gibbon Tool Hire Ltd* are:

$$\text{Daily rate} \quad £4.30$$
$$\text{Weekly rate} \quad £12.60$$

Derek Turner hires it for five complete weeks and for five individual days of different weeks. How much does he pay in hire charges?

Would it have been better for him to have bought a second-hand mixer for £75?

34 HIRE PURCHASE AND MORTGAGES

A. HIRE PURCHASE

Find the deposit payable when the following articles are bought on hire purchase:

	Article	Cash price	Deposit	Cash deposit
1.	Car seat	£120	$\frac{1}{5}$	£120 × $\frac{1}{5}$ = £24
2.	Camera	£250	30%	£250 × $\frac{30}{100}$ = £75
3.	TV set	£344	$\frac{1}{4}$	
4.	Suit	£150	$\frac{1}{3}$	
5.	Freezer	£220	$\frac{1}{5}$	
6.	Caravan	£2600	20%	
7.	Radio cassette recorder	£66	30%	
8.	Tea service	£52	25%	
9.	Central heating system	£1840	10%	
10.	Food processor	£96	$\frac{1}{3}$	

Use the details given below to find the total HP price for each of the following articles. How much would be saved by paying cash?

	Article	Cash price	Deposit	Monthly instalment	Number of instalments due	Total HP price	Amount saved by paying cash
11.	Bicycle	£120	£20	£11	12	£(20 + 11 × 12) = £152	£32
12.	Washing machine	£285	£45	£23	12		
13.	Music centre	£584	£89	£46	12		
14.	TV set	£360	£64.50	£19	18		
15.	Bedroom suite	£1240	$\frac{1}{5}$	£34.50	36		
16.	Leather chair	£360	$\frac{1}{4}$	£14.50	24		
17.	Typewriter	£135	$\frac{1}{3}$	£9.60	12		
18.	Camera	£240	20%	£13.40	18		
19.	Set of drums	£552	25%	£22.50	24		
20.	Greenhouse	£960	30%	£30.52	24		
21.	Carpet	£825	£156	£32.75	24		
22.	Bathroom suite	£1560	10%	£44.78	36		
23.	Electric guitar	£225	$\frac{1}{5}$	£20.16	12		
24.	Motorcycle	£2480	$\frac{1}{4}$	£65.92	36		
25.	Piano	£4995	20%	£134.75	36		

B. BUYING A MOTORCYCLE OR CAR

The table below shows monthly repayments due to a hire purchase company for every £100 borrowed. The deposit is not included.

Rate	Number of instalments				
	12	18	24	30	36
8%	£9	£6.22	£4.88	£4.04	£3.50
10%	£9.20	£6.40	£5.04	£4.24	£3.72
12%	£9.40	£6.62	£5.25	£4.44	£3.93
14%	£9.60	£6.78	£5.46	£4.67	£4.14
16%	£9.75	£6.94	£5.64	£4.88	£4.39

26. David Bowen wishes to buy an £8000 car. If the deposit is 20% what will be his monthly hire purchase repayments if he decides to repay the loan over 30 months when the interest rate is 12%? Find the total cost of the car.

Deposit = £8000 × $\frac{20}{100}$ = £1600

Amount borrowed = £8000 − £1600 = £6400

From the table, the repayment on each £100 borrowed over 30 months at 12% is £4.44 per month. Since £6400 is borrowed:

Monthly repayment = £64 × 4.44 = £284.16
Total of 30 monthly repayments = £284.16 × 30 = £8524.80

Therefore total repayment including deposit = £1600 + £8524.80
= £10 124.80

27. Chris Smith wishes to buy a motorcycle priced £1800. If the deposit is £200, how much will it cost him if he buys on HP over 36 months when the interest rate is 16%?

28. Sue Mizon decides to buy a £20 000 Jaguar car. She pays a deposit of 10% and borrows the remainder when the interest rate is 10%. If she repays over 30 months, how much does the car actually cost her?

29. Chas Morgan decides to buy a £12 000 Sierra. He pays a deposit of $\frac{1}{5}$ and the remainder over 24 months when the interest rate is 14%. How much does the car really cost him?

30. Lois Burley wishes to buy a motorcycle marked £2400. A deposit of $\frac{1}{4}$ is required, the remainder to be paid over 36 months. If the interest rate is 8%, what does the motorcycle actually cost her?

C. MORTGAGES

London Building Society
Calendar Monthly Repayments per £1000 Borrowed

Rate %	Term of years			
	10	15	20	25
10	£13.57	£10.96	£9.79	£9.19
11	£14.16	£11.59	£10.47	£9.90
12	£14.75	£12.24	£11.16	£10.63
13	£15.36	£12.90	£11.87	£11.37
14	£15.98	£13.57	£12.59	£12.13
15	£16.61	£14.26	£13.32	£12.90
16	£17.25	£14.95	£14.06	£13.67
17	£17.89	£15.66	£14.81	£14.46
18	£18.55	£16.37	£15.57	£15.25

Use the above table to find (a) the monthly repayment, (b) the total repayment, on the given borrowed sums of money for the periods stated.

	Name	Sum borrowed	Term of years	Rate %	Monthly repayment	Total repayment
31.	Mr Eyles	£15 000	20	12	£15 × 11.16 = £167.40	£167.40 × 12 × 20 = £40 176
32.	Mr Perry	£10 000	15	13		
33.	Miss Stuart	£14 000	10	18		
34.	Mrs Shortman	£9000	20	14		
35.	Mrs Leeke	£15 000	15	10		
36.	Mr Hoye	£26 000	25	11		
37.	Miss Fears	£32 000	10	15		
38.	Mr Duncan	£40 000	15	16		
39.	Mrs Hart	£45 000	25	18		
40.	Miss Graham	£65 000	20	12		

35 RATES AND RATEABLE VALUE

| Service or Purpose | GLOUCESTERSHIRE COUNTY COUNCIL ||||
| | Gross | Income | Net | Rate/£ |
	£000's	£000's	£000's	p
Education	122 026	19 341	102 685	156.79
School Meals & Milk etc.	5741	2732	3009	4.59
Libraries & Museums	3156	222	2934	4.48
Social Services	20 380	4780	15 600	23.82
Police	23 157	12 474	10 683	16.31
Highways & Local Transport	23 123	8578	14 545	22.21

Calculate the income from a penny rate for each of the following areas:

	Area	Rateable value (RV)	Income from a penny rate
1.	Alford	£2 000 000	2 000 000p = £20 000
2.	Bexeter	£59 400 000	59 400 000p = £594 000
3.	Colworth	£4 600 000	
4.	Daneford	£3 940 000	
5.	Exbran	£6 454 000	
6.	Blackley	£26 400 000	
7.	Minster	£62 940 000	
8.	Lidmouth	£39 700 000	
9.	Totley	£56 470 000	
10.	Waterford	£92 850 000	

The rateable value of Georgetown is £1 200 000. What income will be produced by a rate of:

11. 2p in the £ → 1 200 000 × 2p
 = £24 000

12. 14p in the £ → 1 200 000 × 14p
 = £168 000

13. 23p in the £   15. 42p in the £   17. 60p in the £   19. 84p in the £
14. 30p in the £   16. 53p in the £   18. 67p in the £   20. 120p in the £

Find the rateable value of the given areas if the income from a penny rate is:

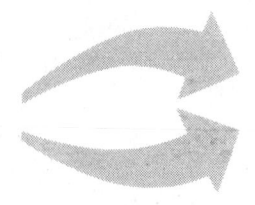

21. Northfield: £4260 → £4260 × 100
 = £426 000

22. Longhill: £37 000
23. Puddletown: £51 700
24. Quink: £42 640
25. Waterford: £12 385
26. Hertfield: £82 850

27. Canford: £126 600
28. Kings Heath: £342 000
29. Vauxhall: £516 420
30. Holland Park: £759 300

Find the rates payable on properties of the given rateable values and for the given rate in the £:

	Rateable value	Rate in £	Rates due
31.	£120	60p	120 × 60p = 7200p = £72
32.	£464	73p	464 × 73p = 33 872p = £338.72
33.	£230	44p	
34.	£350	83p	
35.	£386	67p	
36.	£420	88p	
37.	£646	132p	
38.	£293	120p	
39.	£516	92p	
40.	£720	58p	

Use the given information to calculate the corresponding rate in the £:

	Rateable value	Rates due	Rate in £
41.	£400	£200	£ $\dfrac{200}{400}$ = £0.5 = 50p
42.	£350	£220.50	£ $\dfrac{220.50}{350}$ = £0.63 = 63p
43.	£260	£208	
44.	£380	£247	
45.	£490	£357.70	
46.	£375	£217.50	
47.	£248	£272.80	
48.	£650	£858	
49.	£760	£592.80	
50.	£888	£612.72	

Find the rateable value of the properties on which the following rates are due for the given rate in the £:

	Rates due	Rate in £	Rateable value
51.	£156	60p	£ $\dfrac{156 \times 100}{60}$ = £260
52.	£250.88	49p	£ $\dfrac{250.88 \times 100}{49}$ = £512
53.	£308	70p	
54.	£382.80	66p	
55.	£257.30	83p	
56.	£244.72	92p	
57.	£725.76	108p	
58.	£949.76	112p	
59.	£525.36	88p	
60.	£581.25	93p	

61. Tom Rees lives in a house in Gloucester with a rateable value of £315 and pays rates of 76p in the £, while his brother lives in Cheltenham in a house with a rateable value of £286 but pays rates of 81p in the £. Which brother pays the larger amount, and by how much?

119

62. Miss Collins pays £246.96 in a year when the rate in the £ is 84p. Find the RV of her house. How much will she pay next year if the rate in the £ is increased by 8p?

63. Miss Robinson and Miss Deats live in flats with rateable values of £388 and £424 respectively. If Miss Deats pays £24.12 more in rates than Miss Robinson, find the rate in the £ and the amount paid in rates by each.

64. The total rateable value of Manpool is £3 672 000. Find the income from a penny rate. If a rate of 39.5p in the £ is required to meet the cost of education, how much is spent each year on this service?
I live in Manpool in a house with a rateable value of £244. How much will I contribute towards the cost of education?

65. I pay £162.80 in rates on my house which has a rateable value of £296, but when I improve the property the council raises my rateable value by £44. What is the rate in the £? How much should I pay next year if the rate in the £ is 65p?

66. When the rate in the pound is 86p I pay £213.28 in rates. Find the rateable value of my house. If a rate of 18.4p in the £ is spent on Social Services how much do I contribute to these in a year?

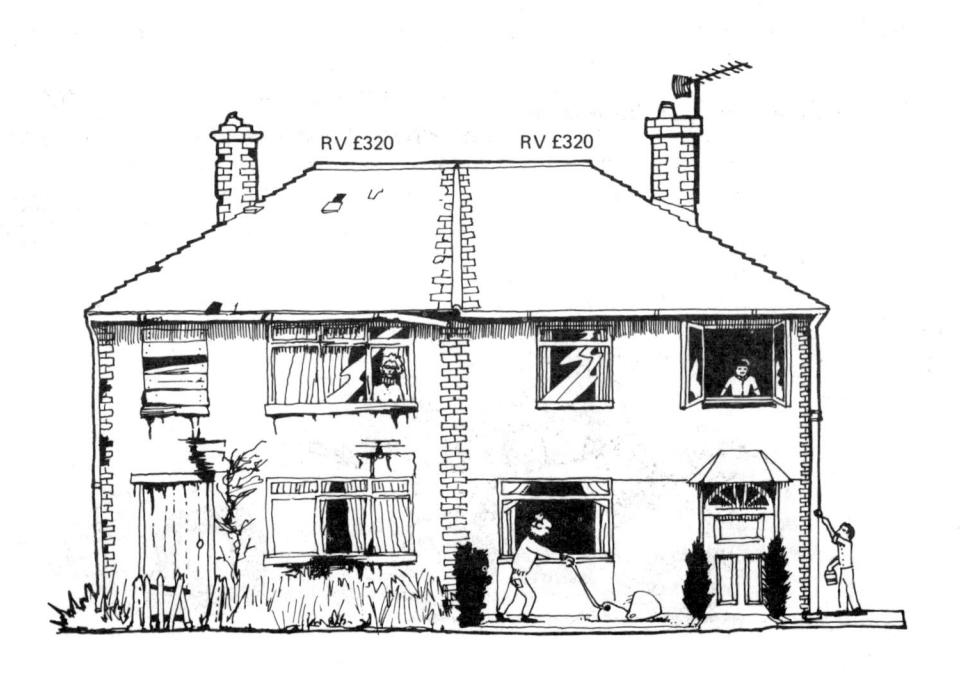

36 COST OF RUNNING A MOTORCYCLE OR CAR

1. Sarah's motorcycle expenses for a year were: Road tax £36, Insurance £174, Depreciation (decrease in value) £300, Fuel: 1000 litres at 45p per litre, Servicing and repairs £40.
   Calculate:
   (a) the cost of fuel
   (b) the total costs for the year
   (c) the average cost per kilometre if she travels 20 km on each litre.

   (a) Cost of fuel = 1000 × 45p = £450

   (b) Total costs for the year = £36 + £174 + £300 + £450 + £40 = £1000

   (c) Average cost per kilometre = $\dfrac{\text{total costs}}{\text{number of km travelled}}$ = £$\dfrac{1000}{20 \times 1000}$

   $ = \dfrac{100\,000}{20 \times 1000}$p

   $ = 5p$

Use the given information to find for each person: (a) the total fuel cost, (b) the total costs, (c) the number of km (or miles) travelled in the year, (d) the average cost per kilometre (or per mile).

	Name	Road tax	Insurance	Depreciation	Fuel	Number of km/litre	Servicing and repairs
2.	Peter	£18	£72	£180	1200 litres at 40p/litre	20	£50
3.	Sally	£10	£140	£370	1600 litres at 50p/litre	22	£88
4.	Ali	£9	£70	£280	1450 litres at 42p/litre	24	£76
5.	Keri	£36	£124	£450	1350 litres at 40p/litre	18	£65
6.	Bruno	£10	£185	£450	1800 litres at 72p/litre	25	£84
7.	Vicki	£30	£244	£400	1500 litres at 60p/litre	22	£76
8.	Mandy	£40	£858	£562	1320 litres at 55p/litre	18	£190
9.	Fred	£20	£320	£404	840 litres at 45p/litre	20	£54
10.	David	£25	£485	£420	970 litres at 50p/litre	25	£137

	Name	Road tax	Insurance	Depreciation	Fuel	Number of miles/gallon	Servicing and repairs
11.	Joan	£50	£200	£900	300 gallons at £2/gallon	30	£50
12.	Pat	£40	£300	£1300	400 gallons at £2/gallon	35	£80
13.	Ahmed	£20	£440	£1100	450 gallons at £2.30/gallon	40	£105
14.	Sean	£15	£100	£600	200 gallons at £2.20/gallon	60	£45
15.	Olive	£25	£150	£850	370 gallons at £1.95/gallon	48	£118.30

37 LIFE ASSURANCE

Age	Premium		Age	Premium	
	Man	Woman		Man	Woman
21	£5.05	£4.80	36	£6.50	£6.14
22	£5.10	£4.85	37	£6.65	£6.28
23	£5.15	£4.90	38	£6.70	£6.42
24	£5.20	£4.95	39	£6.86	£6.58
25	£5.25	£5.00	40	£7.02	£6.74
26	£5.31	£5.06	41	£7.20	£6.92
27	£5.37	£5.12	42	£7.38	£7.10
28	£5.43	£5.20	43	£7.60	£7.34
29	£5.51	£5.28	44	£7.86	£7.60
30	£5.61	£5.38	45	£8.17	£7.90
31	£5.73	£5.50	46	£8.58	£8.30
32	£5.95	£5.62	47	£9.08	£8.80
33	£6.07	£5.74	48	£9.30	£9.40
34	£6.19	£5.86	49	£10.42	£10.10
35	£6.33	£6.00	50	£11.25	£10.90

The table shows the yearly premium for men and women between 21 years and 50 years for each £100 assured.

1. Find the premium due on the life of a 29-year-old man assured for £10 000.

   From the table, premium for £100 assured for a 29-year-old man is £5.51. ∴ premium for £10 000

   $= £5.51 \times \dfrac{10\ 000}{100}$

   $= £551$

2. A woman aged 40 takes out a life assurance policy for £8000. Find her yearly premium.

   Premium for each £100 assured for a 40-year-old woman is £6.74. ∴ premium for £8000

   $= £6.74 \times \dfrac{8000}{100}$

   $= £539.20$

Find the yearly premium due for each of the following policies:

	Name	Age	Amount assured
3.	Miss Black	26	£1000
4.	Mr John	34	£2000
5.	Mrs Short	29	£5000
6.	Mr Khan	41	£7000
7.	Miss King	37	£8000
8.	Mr Marples	28	£9000
9.	Mrs Lodge	43	£12 000
10.	Mr Brown	48	£15 000

In the following questions find the yearly premium due for the amounts assured and hence find the monthly premium, giving your answers correct to the nearest penny:

	Name	Age	Amount assured
11.	Mr Green	37	£2000
12.	Miss Collins	44	£5000
13.	Mrs Stuart	23	£8000
14.	Miss Deans	26	£10 000
15.	Mr Leslie	32	£7500

38 SIMPLE AND COMPOUND INTEREST

Use your calculator to find the simple interest on:

1. £100 for 3 years at 8%
$$= £\frac{100 \times 8 \times 3}{100} = £24$$

2. £430 for 4 years at 12%
$$= £\frac{430 \times 12 \times 4}{100} = £206.40$$

3. £276.44 for 3 years at 11%
$$= £\frac{276.44 \times 11 \times 3}{100} = £91.2252$$
$$= £91.23$$

4. £634 for 5 months at 14%
$$= £\frac{634 \times 14 \times 5}{100 \times 12} = £36.983333$$
$$= £36.98$$

5. £200 for 4 years at 9%
6. £600 for 3 years at 10%
7. £700 for 4 years at 8%
8. £550 for 6 years at 12%
9. £430 for 7 years at 14%
10. £870 for 4 years at 16%
11. £910 for 3 years at 15%
12. £145 for 5 months at 8%
13. £265 for 9 months at 9%
14. £316 for 15 months at $8\frac{1}{2}$%

15. £198 for 5 years at $7\frac{1}{2}$%
16. £254 for 7 years at 14%
17. £360.40 for 4 years at 12%
18. £165.55 for 5 years at 13%
19. £282.64 for $4\frac{1}{2}$ years at 11%
20. £648.29 for $3\frac{1}{2}$ years at 9%

Use your calculator to find the compound interest on:

21. £300 for 2 years at 12%
   $= £300 \times 1.12 \times 1.12$
   $= £376.32$
   $\therefore$ C.I. $= £376.32 - £300 = £76.32$

22. £424 for 3 years at 14%
   $= £424 \times 1.14 \times 1.14 \times 1.14$
   $= £628.17465 = £628.17$
   $\therefore$ C.I. $= £628.17 - £424$
   $= £204.17$

23. £520 for 2 years at 10%
24. £850 for 2 years at 11%
25. £484 for 2 years at 12%
26. £137 for 2 years at 14%
27. £328 for 2 years at 15%
28. £273 for 2 years at 18%
29. £98 for 3 years at 20%
30. £565 for 3 years at 14%

Graph to show how £1 grows at different rates of compound interest

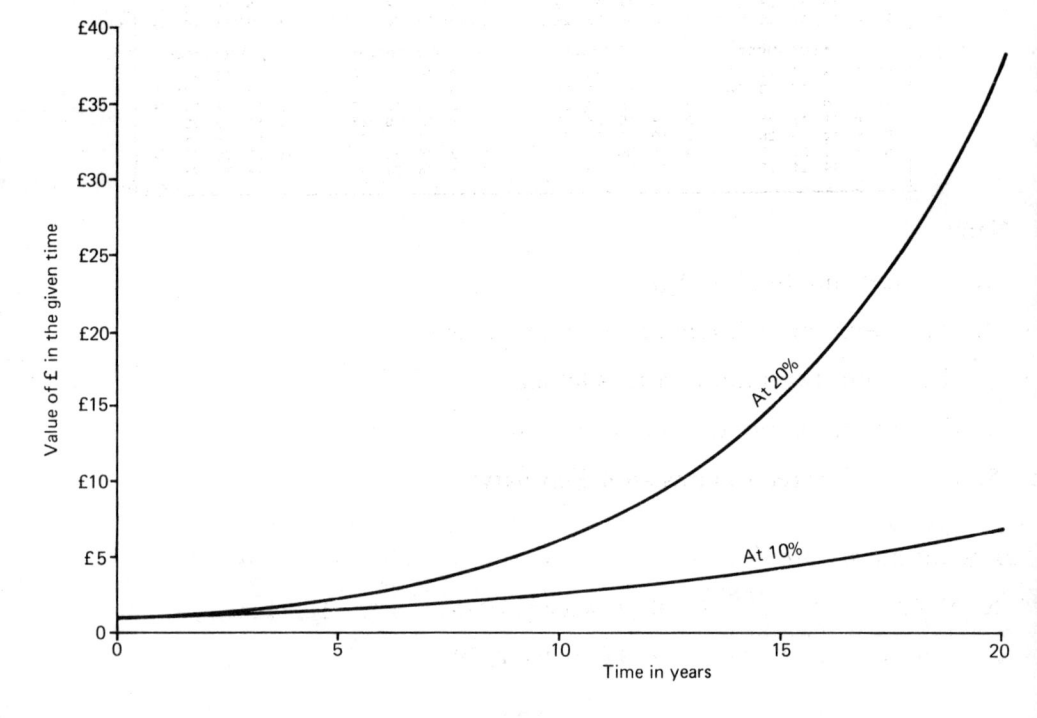

39 THE CALENDAR, TIME AND TIME ZONES

A. THE CALENDAR

	January	February	1986 March	April
M	6 13 20 27	3 10 17 24	3 10 17 24 31	7 14 21 28
T	7 14 21 28	4 11 18 25	4 11 18 25	1 8 15 22 29
W	1 8 15 22 29	5 12 19 26	5 12 19 26	2 9 16 23 30
T	2 9 16 23 30	6 13 20 27	6 13 20 27	3 10 17 24
F	3 10 17 24 31	7 14 21 28	7 14 21 28	4 11 18 25
S	4 11 18 25	1 8 15 22	1 8 15 22 29	5 12 19 26
S	5 12 19 26	2 9 16 23	2 9 16 23 30	6 13 20 27
	May	**June**	**July**	**August**
M	5 12 19 26	2 9 16 23 30	7 14 21 28	4 11 18 25
T	6 13 20 27	3 10 17 24	1 8 15 22 29	5 12 19 26
W	7 14 21 28	4 11 18 25	2 9 16 23 30	6 13 20 27
T	1 8 15 22 29	5 12 19 26	3 10 17 24 31	7 14 21 28
F	2 9 16 23 30	6 13 20 27	4 11 18 25	1 8 15 22 29
S	3 10 17 24 31	7 14 21 28	5 12 19 26	2 9 16 23 30
S	4 11 18 25	1 8 15 22 29	6 13 20 27	3 10 17 24 31
	September	**October**	**November**	**December**
M	1 8 15 22 29	6 13 20 27	3 10 17 24	1 8 15 22 29
T	2 9 16 23 30	7 14 21 28	4 11 18 25	2 9 16 23 30
W	3 10 17 24	1 8 15 22 29	5 12 19 26	3 10 17 24 31
T	4 11 18 25	2 9 16 23 30	6 13 20 27	4 11 18 25
F	5 12 19 26	3 10 17 24 31	7 14 21 28	5 12 19 26
S	6 13 20 27	4 11 18 25	1 8 15 22 29	6 13 20 27
S	7 14 21 28	5 12 19 26	2 9 16 23 30	7 14 21 28

Name:

1. the next month after April
2. the month immediately before September
3. the month two months after October
4. the month six months before August
5. the month three months after February

How many days are there in:

6. March
7. November
8. February 1988
9. February 1989
10. June

127

June						
Mon	Tues	Wed	Thurs	Fri	Sat	Sun
					1	2
3	4	5	6	7	8	9
10	11	12	13	14	15	16
17	18	19	20	21	22	23
24	25	26	27	28	29	30

Today is Friday 14 June. What date was it:

11. last Sunday
12. last Tuesday
13. a week last Wednesday
14. two weeks yesterday
15. ten days ago

Today is Wednesday 5 June. What date will it be:

16. next Tuesday
17. next Saturday
18. on Thursday week
19. a week next Wednesday
20. four weeks today

August					
S		6	13	20	27
M		7	14	21	28
Tu	1	8	15	22	29
W	2	9	16	23	30
Th	3	10	17	24	31
F	4	11	18	25	
S	5	12	19	26	

Today is Tuesday 8 August. What date will it be:

21. next Sunday
22. the day after tomorrow
23. a week Thursday
24. three weeks today
25. in twelve days' time

Today is Sunday 20 August. What date was it:

26. last Sunday
27. a week yesterday
28. the day before yesterday
29. three weeks ago today
30. ten days ago

B. TIME

Write down the time shown on each of the following clock faces:

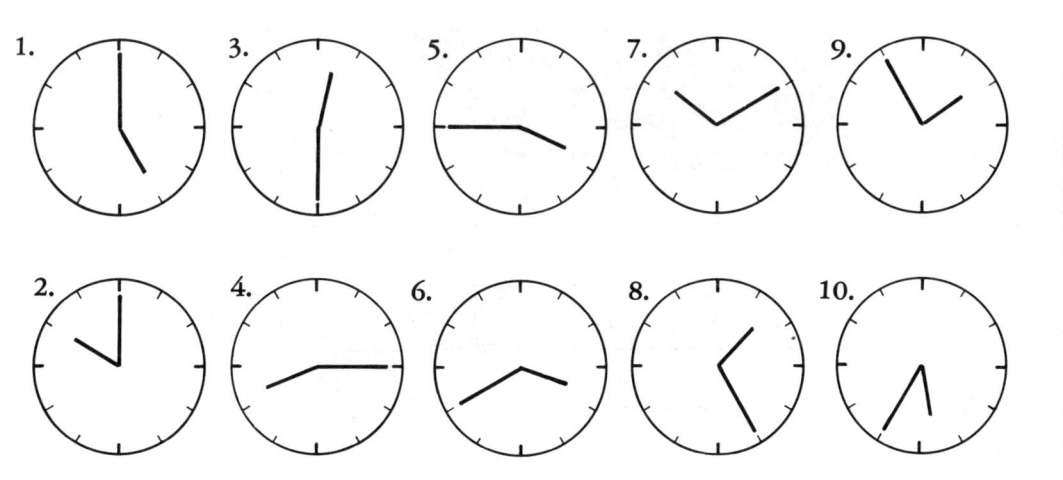

Complete the following tables

	24 hour clock time	am/pm time	Time in words
11.	0215	2.15 am	Quarter past two in the morning
12.	1525	3.25 pm	Twenty-five past three in the afternoon
13.	0442	4.42 am	Eighteen minutes to five in the morning
14.	1835	6.35 pm	Twenty-five to seven in the evening
15.	0520		
16.	0218		
17.	1325		
18.	2006		
19.	0742		
20.	1551		
21.		3.15 am	
22.		9.24 am	
23.		7.27 pm	
24.		6.54 am	
25.		4.43 pm	
26.			Ten past one in the morning
27.			Twenty-four minutes past ten in the morning
28.			Six minutes past five in the afternoon
29.			Sixteen minutes to twelve in the morning
30.			Seven minutes to midnight

How many hours and minutes are there between the following times?

31. 0900 and 1100
32. 0700 and 1500
33. 0230 and 0854
34. 0422 and 1647
35. 0547 and 0732
36. 0256 and 1512
37. 1359 and 1642
38. 3.56 am and 1.42 pm
39. 10.42 am and 8.19 pm
40. 4.12 am and 7.33 pm

Complete the following table which gives details of journeys between various places:

	Time of departure	Time of arrival	Length of journey
41.	10.32	12.27	1 h 55 min
42.	0446	0854	
43.	1321	1618	
44.	0327	1550	
45.	0754		32 min
46.	1519		2 h 8 min
47.	0236		14 h 38 min
48.		1241	45 min
49.		0927	3 h 45 min
50.		1657	13 h 4 min

51.

The clock shows the time that Betty finished school.

(a) What time did she arrive at home if it was 35 minutes after school finished?

(b) She started her lunch break 3 h 35 min earlier than the time shown on the clock. What time was this?

(c) Find the length of her school day if she arrived in school at 9.05 am

(d) In the afternoon she had three lessons each of 35 minutes but no break. What time did each lesson start?

(e) How long was morning school?

130

52. Below is the timetable for a school day:

Registration	8.45 am
Assembly	8.55 am
First lesson	9.15 am
Second lesson	9.50 am
Third lesson	10.25 am
Morning break	11.00 am
Fourth lesson	11.15 am
Fifth lesson	11.50 am
Dinner break	12.25 pm
Afternoon registration	1.35 pm
Sixth lesson	1.40 pm
Seventh lesson	2.20 pm
Eighth lesson	3.00 pm
School ends	3.40 pm

(a) How long is assembly?

(b) How long is the morning break?

(c) How long is the school day?

(d) How long is the dinner break?

(e) What is the total lesson time in the morning?

(f) What is the total lesson time in the afternoon?

(g) What length of time in the school day is not used for lessons?

C. TIME ZONES

The map on page 132 is a *simplified* version of how the world is divided into time zones. In places to the east the sun rises *earlier* than for us — their day starts *before* ours. For places west of us, i.e. the Americas, the sun rises *later* than it does for us — their day starts *after* ours.
Use the information on the map to answer the following questions. You may also like to discover the country each place is in.

1. How many hours is New York time ahead or behind London time?

   New York is 5 time divisions to the west of London, i.e. New York time is 5 hours behind London time.

2. How does Calcutta time differ from time in (a) London, (b) Jerusalem, (c) Hong Kong?

3. How does the time in Aden compare with the time in (a) Cairo, (b) Perth, (c) Tokyo?

THE WORLD

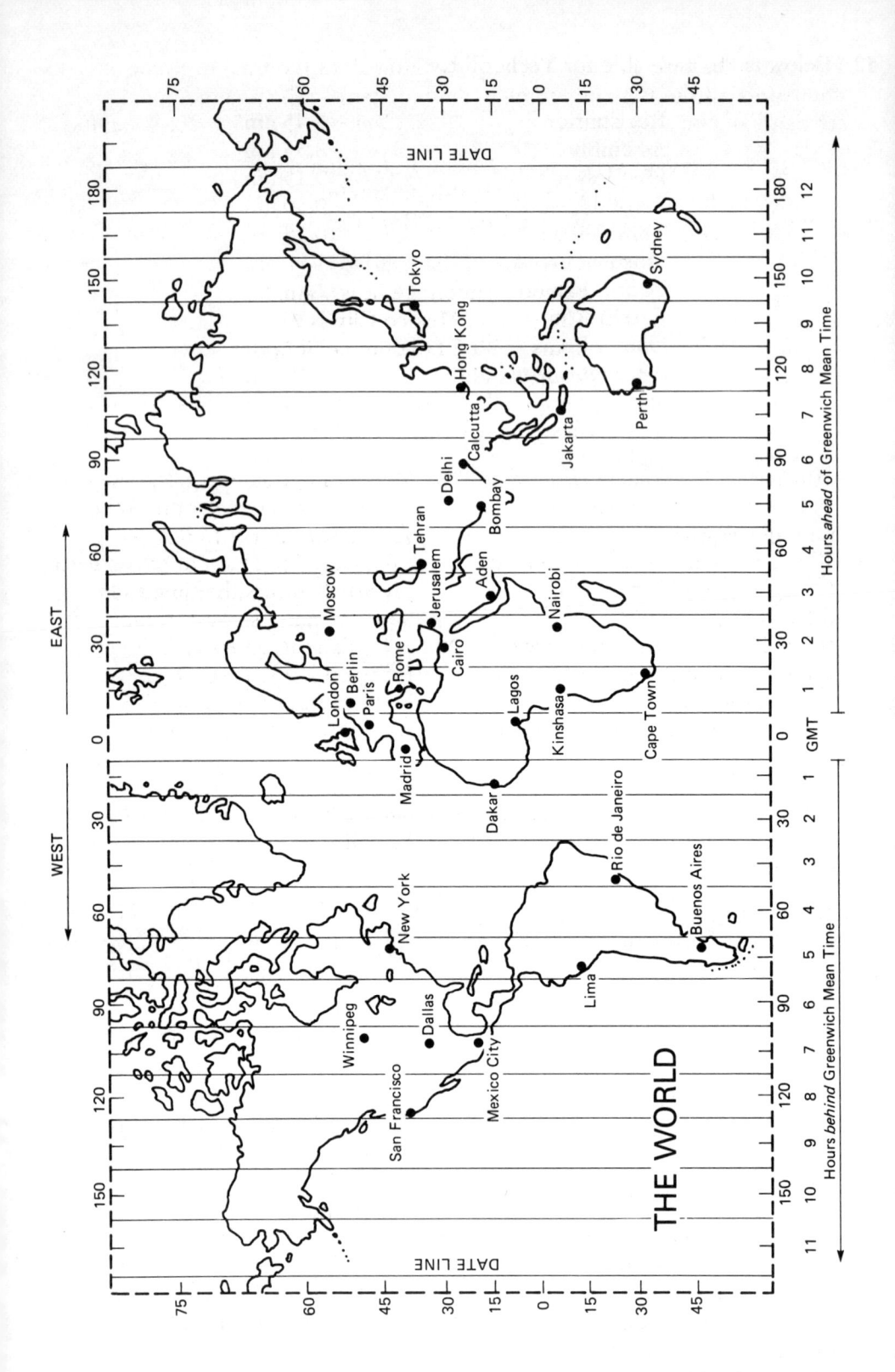

4. How does the time in New York compare with the time in (a) Lima, (b) San Francisco, (c) Dallas?
5. How does the time in Rome compare with the time in (a) Tehran, (b) Perth, (c) Winnipeg?
6. When it is 12 noon in London what time is it in (a) Rio de Janeiro, (b) Mexico City, (c) Bombay?

   (a) The time in Rio is 3 hours behind London, i.e. it is 9 am.
   (b) The time in Mexico City is 7 hours behind London, i.e. it is 5 am.
   (c) The time in Bombay is 5 hours ahead of London, i.e. it is 5 pm.

7. When it is 12 noon in London what time is it in (a) Paris, (b) Lagos, (c) Cape Town?
8. When it is 12 noon in London what time is it in (a) Hong Kong, (b) Tokyo, (c) Sydney?
9. When it is 12 noon in London what time is it in (a) Aden, (b) Buenos Aires, (c) Kinshasa?
10. When it is 4 pm in London what time is it in (a) New York, (b) Perth, (c) Lima?
11. When it is 6 am in London what time is it in (a) Lima, (b) Cairo, (c) Delhi?
12. When it is 12 noon in Aden what time is it in (a) Bombay, (b) Jakarta, (c) Tokyo?
13. When it is 12 noon in Bombay what time is it in (a) Cairo, (b) Madrid (c) Perth?
14. When it is 6 pm in Lima what time is it in (a) Dallas, (b) Dakar, (c) Moscow?
15. When it is 10 am in Cairo what time is it in (a) Delhi, (b) New York, (c) Tokyo?
16. When it is 1600 in Madrid what time is it in (a) Jakarta, (b) Winnipeg, (c) Berlin?
17. What time is it in (a) Lagos, (b) Calcutta, (c) San Francisco, when it is 0800 in Nairobi?
18. My cousin in Sydney telephones me at 11 am Sydney time. Where should she expect to find me?
19. I telephone my aunt in Dallas when my watch shows the time to be 9 pm. Is this a sensible thing to do?
20. A firm's representative in Jakarta telephoned the head office in London at 1700 on a weekday. Should he expect a reply?
21. John got up at 6 am to listen to a commentary on a football match being played in the north island of New Zealand. What time was it there?
22. Jackie stayed up to listen to a commentary on the Olympic Games from San Francisco. If it was 4 pm there, what time was it in London?
23. Play for the day in the Perth Test Match finished at 6.30 pm. What time was this in London?
24. When Peter Verney switched on for the 8 am breakfast show in Dallas, what time was it in Edinburgh?
25. The Tokyo marathon started at 8 am. What time would I need to switch on my TV set in Cardiff to watch it live?

40 BUS AND TRAIN TIMETABLES

Timetable A
Antford–Peterwood

ANTFORD	dep	0620	0830	0930	1045	1205	1535	1720	2035
BEWLEY	dep	0623	0833	0933	1048	1208	1538	1723	2038
CATMINSTER	dep	0629	0839	0939	1054	1214	1544	1729	2044
DOWN TOWN	dep	0632	0842	0942	1057	1217	1547	1732	2047
EDGEHILL	dep	0636	0846	0946	1101	1221	1551	1736	2051
FOXBOROUGH	dep	0642	0852	0952	1107	1227	1557	1742	2057
GAUNT	dep	0646	0856	0956	1111	1231	1601	1746	2101
HUCKLETON	dep	0649	0859	0959	1114	1234	1604	1749	2104
ILKLEY	dep	0655	0905	1005	1120	1240	1610	1755	2110
JENNER	dep	0700	0910	1010	1125	1245	1615	1800	2115
KNIGHTON	dep	0703	0913	1013	1128	1248	1618	1803	2118
LOXSTOW	dep	0708	0918	1018	1133	1253	1623	1808	2123
MANDOVER	dep	0711	0921	1021	1136	1256	1626	1811	2126
NUTFORD	dep	0714	0924	1024	1139	1259	1629	1814	2129
OVERVILLE	dep	—	—	1030	1145	1305	1635	1820	—
PETERWOOD	arr	0722	0932	1033	1148	1308	1638	1823	2137

Use timetable A, which gives details of buses travelling from Antford to Peterwood, to answer the following questions:

1. How long does the 0830 from Antford take to get to Peterwood?
2. How many buses do not stop at Overville?
3. How long does the 1535 from Antford take to travel from Edgehill to Peterwood?
4. How long does it take to travel from Catminster to Loxstow?
5. I arrive at the bus stop in Gaunt at 1545. What time should I arrive in Peterwood?
6. What is the latest time I can leave Jenner to arrive in Peterwood by 1030?
7. What is the latest time I can leave Bewley to arrive in Knighton by 1715?
8. I arrived in Peterwood at 1638. What time did I board the bus at Huckleton?
9. I arrived in Nutford at 0924. What time did I pass through Foxborough?
10. Tom must be in Overville by 2120. What time should he leave Jenner?

134

Timetable B
Train times to London

ABER	dep	—	—	—	—	—	—	—	—	—	0700	0755	—	—	—	—	0950	—
RAYNE	dep	—	—	—	—	—	—	—	—	—	0727	0827	—	0933	—	—	1125	—
WOOLMER	dep	—	—	—	—	—	—	—	—	—	0745	0845	—	0951	—	—	1143	—
KIRTON	dep	—	—	—	—	—	—	—	—	—	0700	—	—	—	1002	—	1106	—
HOLT	dep	—	—	—	—	—	—	—	—	—	0730	—	—	—	1035	—	1131	—
ESTON	dep	—	—	—	—	0525	—	0643	0735	—	0835	0928	—	1038	1128	—	1228	—
BUCKFAST	dep	—	—	—	—	0554	—	0706	0803	—	0859	0959	—	1103	1159	—	1259	—
SUNLAW	dep	—	—	—	0605	0630	0705	0730	0830	—	0930	1030	—	1130	1230	—	1330	1430
GAROD	dep	—	—	—	0617	0642	0717	0742	0842	—	0942	1042	—	1142	1242	—	1342	1442
DANEHILL	dep	—	—	—	0624	0649	0724	0749	0849	—	0949	1049	—	1149	1249	—	1349	1449
ALNE	dep	—	—	—	0635	0700	0735	0800	0900	—	1000	1100	—	1200	1300	—	1400	1500
TETNEY	dep	0430	0555	0630	0700	0725	0800	0825	0925	0935	1025	1125	1157	1225	1325	1357	1425	1525
LANGOLD	dep	0444	0606	0641	0713	0738	0813	0838	0938	0947	1038	1138	1210	1238	1338	1410	1438	1538
CROSSWELL	dep	0513	0626	0701	0733	0758	0833	0858	—	1011	1058	—	1230	1258	—	1430	1458	1558
PLUCKTON	dep	0549	0654	0732	0800	—	0901	—	—	1047	—	—	1258	—	—	1458	—	—
GREENFORD	dep	0655	0711	—	0851	—	—	—	—	1107	—	—	1315	—	—	1515	—	—
RIBBY	dep	0623	0727	0800	—	0849	—	0949	—	1124	1149	—	1332	1349	—	1532	1549	1649
PULHAM	dep	0712	0800	0840	—	0952	—	1052	—	1142	1246	—	1346	1446	—	1546	1642	1742
LONDON	arr	0700	0756	0830	0855	0918	0953	1018	1109	1203	1218	1309	1405	1418	1509	1605	1616	1718

Use Timetable B, which gives train times from Aber, and intermediate stations, to London, to answer the following questions:

11. How many trains are there from Aber to London?
12. How many trains are there from Sunlaw to London?
13. How many trains are there from Tetney to London?
14. What is the earliest I can leave Garod to go to London? What time should I arrive?
15. How long does the 0705 from Sunlaw take to get to London?
16. How many trains stop at Pluckton?
17. Sally leaves Woolmer at 0845. What time will she arrive in London?
18. George lives at Crosswell and wishes to travel to London arriving there before 1230. What time should he leave?
19. How long does the 0643 from Eston take to travel between Alne and Pulham?
20. I arrive at Langold ten minutes late for the 0738. How long must I wait for the next train?
21. Jane arrives in Buckfast fifteen minutes late for the 0859. How long must she wait for the next train?
22. On which train should I leave Eston to get to Crosswell by 1240?
23. On which train should I leave Danehill to get to Pulham by 1450?
24. On which train should I leave Sunlaw to get to Pulham by 1130?
25. How many trains pass through Tetney before 0800?
26. How many stops does the 0735 from Eston make on its trip to London?
27. How many stops does the 1002 from Kirton make on its trip to London?
28. How long does the 0755 from Aber take to travel to Tetney?
29. How long does the 1002 from Kirton take to travel from Sunlaw to London?
30. How long does the 0643 from Eston take to travel from Danehill to Ribby?

135

41 PACKAGE HOLIDAYS

The table opposite gives the prices per person for holidays in the Spanish resort of Calella. Use this table to answer the questions that follow:

1. Which hotel appears to be the most expensive?
2. Which hotel is the cheapest?
3. How much would a two-week holiday for two cost at the Hotel Agustina leaving on 26 August?
4. How much would a one-week holiday for two cost at the Hotel Excelsior leaving Britain on 24 July? Find the deposit.
5. How much would a two-week holiday at the Hotel Gabriela cost two adults if they start their holiday on 18 September? Find the deposit.
6. How much would a two-week holiday for three adults at the Hotel Llonga cost if the holiday begins on 8 April? Find the deposit.
7. How much would a three-week holiday for two cost at the Hotel Montana commencing on 16 May?
8. What would a three-week holiday for three adults cost at the Hotel Miguel if the holiday starts on 1 August?
9. What would be the cost of a two-week holiday for a family of four — father, mother and two children aged 5 years and 8 years — at the Hotel Vadella if they leave for their holiday on 24 May?
10. If I leave for my holiday on Saturday 10 July, which hotel gives me the cheapest one-week holiday?
11. If I leave for a two-week holiday on Saturday 20 August, which hotel gives me the most expensive holiday?
12. What would be the cancellation charge for the holiday referred to in question 4 if it was cancelled 40 days before it was due to start?
13. What would be the cancellation charge for the holiday referred to in question 5 if it was cancelled 20 days before it was due to start?
14. What would be the cancellation charge for the holiday referred to in question 6 if it was cancelled a week before it was due to start?
15. How much would a two-week holiday (leaving on 10 July) at the Hotel Pueblo cost Mr Tucker for a family of five — Mr and Mrs Tucker plus their children aged 6, 11 and 14 years? How much would they have to pay in deposits?
16. John and Betty Robinson take their 3-year-old son on a holiday at the Hotel Agustina, leaving on 3 September. Find the total cost if they stay for three weeks. How much deposit would be required?

Prices per person in £

Saturday departures on or between these dates	20 April–17 May			8–19 April 25 May–12 July			18–24 May 14 Sept–31 Oct			24 Aug–13 Sept			13 July–23 Aug		
Hotel	1 wk	2 wks	extra wk	1 wk	2 wks	extra wk	1 wk	2 wks	extra wk	1 wk	2 wks	extra wk	1 wk	2 wks	extra wk
Llonga	241	293	50	257	314	54	269	330	59	283	359	74	293	370	74
Agustina	233	277	42	248	296	46	259	311	49	270	334	62	281	344	52
Excelsior	227	267	37	242	285	40	253	298	43	262	317	54	273	327	54
Vadella	235	281	43	251	301	50	263	316	52	274	340	68	282	349	68
Pueblo	228	268	37	243	286	42	254	300	44	263	318	59	271	328	57
Montana	223	259	33	238	276	38	249	289	39	255	304	52	263	314	50
Gabriela	252	328	66	270	352	73	283	371	78	300	405	96	310	416	96
Miguel	258	308	45	273	326	50	284	340	52	293	358	67	301	368	65

Child reductions (2–11 inclusive): 20%; children under 2 years: free
Deposit: £50 per person; £30 for children 2–11
Cancellation charge: more than 56 days before departure 30%;
15–56 days 40%, 1–14 days 50%

17. Dr Roman sends his three children aged 12, 14 and 16 years on holiday for two weeks at the Hotel Pueblo, leaving on 6 July. How much will it cost him?

18. Clarrie Layne takes his two children aged 14 and 18 years for a three-week holiday at the Hotel Excelsior. How much will it cost him if the holiday starts on 8 August? How much would the deposit be?

19. Syd Millar books a two-week holiday for himself, his wife and four children aged 7, 9, 11 and 13 years, at the Hotel Montana, leaving on 26 August. Two months before the departure date he finds that they are all unable to go. Find the cancellation charge.

20. A family of four — father, mother and two children aged 8 and 10 years — wish to take a two-week holiday. Which is the cheaper, and by how much: Hotel Agustina leaving on 28 April or Hotel Vadella leaving on 16 July?

42 FOREIGN CURRENCY

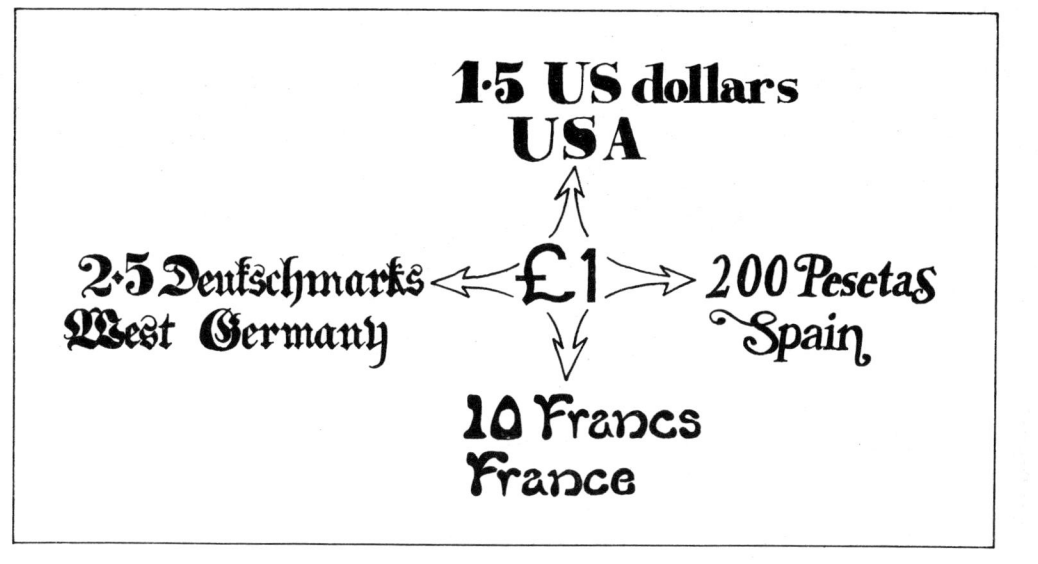

1·5 US dollars USA

2·5 Deutschmarks West Germany ← **£1** → **200 Pesetas** Spain

10 Francs France

Use the above exchange rates to find:

1. £2 in francs = 2 × 10 francs
   = 20 f

2. £3 in pesetas
3. £4 in Deutschmarks
4. £2 in dollars
5. £6 in Deutschmarks
6. £5 in francs
7. £8 in pesetas
8. £50 in dollars
9. 400 pta in pounds
10. $30 in pounds
11. 60 f in pounds
12. 25 DM in pounds

If £1 ≡ 10 f and £1 ≡ 200 pta, convert the following amounts into (a) French francs, (b) Spanish pesetas:

13. £20 is (a) 20 × 10 f = 200 f
    (b) 20 × 200 pta = 4000 pta

14. £30
15. £50
16. £80
17. £110
18. £150
19. £200
20. £300
21. £500
22. £850
23. £75
24. £160
25. £320
26. £432
27. £573

Use the same exchange rates to convert the following amounts into pounds:

28. 150 f = £$\frac{150}{10}$ = £15

29. 750 pta = £$\frac{750}{200}$ = £3.75

30. 200 f
31. 550 f
32. 760 f
33. 436 f
34. 829 f
35. 1234 f
36. 339 f
37. 5379 f
38. 600 pta
39. 8000 pta
40. 7500 pta
41. 12 500 pta
42. 2350 pta
43. 6760 pta
44. 8930 pta
45. 15 400 pta

Use the following exchange rates to convert the given amounts into the various foreign currencies:

	Amount in £	Country	Monetary unit	Rate of exchange, i.e. value of £1	Equivalent value in foreign currency
46.	50	West Germany	Deutschmark	3 DM	50 × 3 DM = 150 DM
47.	80	Portugal	escudo	120 escudos	80 × 120 escudos = 9600 escudos
48.	60	Italy	lira	2100 L	
49.	70	USA	dollar	$1.5	
50.	100	USA	dollar	$1.4	
51.	300	Sweden	krona	10 krona	
52.	250	Denmark	kroner	12.4 kroner	
53.	75	Italy	lira	2300 L	
54.	360	Austria	schilling	30 schillings	
55.	425	USA	dollar	$1.48	

Use the following exchange rates to convert the given amounts into pounds:

	Amount	Country	Rate of exchange, i.e. value of £1	Equivalent value in £
56.	$66	USA	$1.5	$£\dfrac{66}{1.5} = £44$
57.	140 400 L	Italy	1800 L	$£\dfrac{140\,400}{1800} = £78$
58.	5040 dr	Greece	120 dr	
59.	4620 pta	Spain	140 pta	
60.	3388 Y	Japan	220 Y	
61.	9280 f	Belgium	80 f	
62.	183 f	France	12.2 f	
63.	$257 HK	Hong Kong	$4 HK	
64.	238 DM	West Germany	2.8 DM	
65.	2392 escudos	Portugal	130 escudos	

66. A bicycle costs 1452 f in a shop in Paris. What would be the equivalent price in pounds if 12 f ≡ £1?
67. A record costs 10 944 L in Rome. What would be the equivalent price in pounds if £1 ≡ 2400 lira?
68. A leather case which sells in Malaga for 2952 pta is to be sold in Glasgow. What would be the equivalent price if £1 ≡ 180 pta?
69. How much would a meal costing £9.40 in London cost in Bonn, West Germany, if £1 ≡ 2.85 DM?
70. A bottle of perfume sells for $51.62 in New York. What would be the equivalent price in London if £1 ≡ $1.45?

43 APPRECIATION AND DEPRECIATION (INCREASE AND DECREASE IN VALUE)

1. Paul's house increases in value by 10% each year. If he bought it for £20 000, what would it be worth in (a) 3 years, (b) 5 years?

   (a) Purchase price = £20 000
   Value after 1 year
   = £20 000 × 1.10 = £22 000
   Value after 2 years
   = £22 000 × 1.10 = £24 000
   Value after 3 years
   = £24 200 × 1.10 = £26 620

   (b) Value after 4 years
   = £26 620 × 1.10 = £29 282
   Value after 5 years
   = £29 282 × 1.10
   = £32 210.20

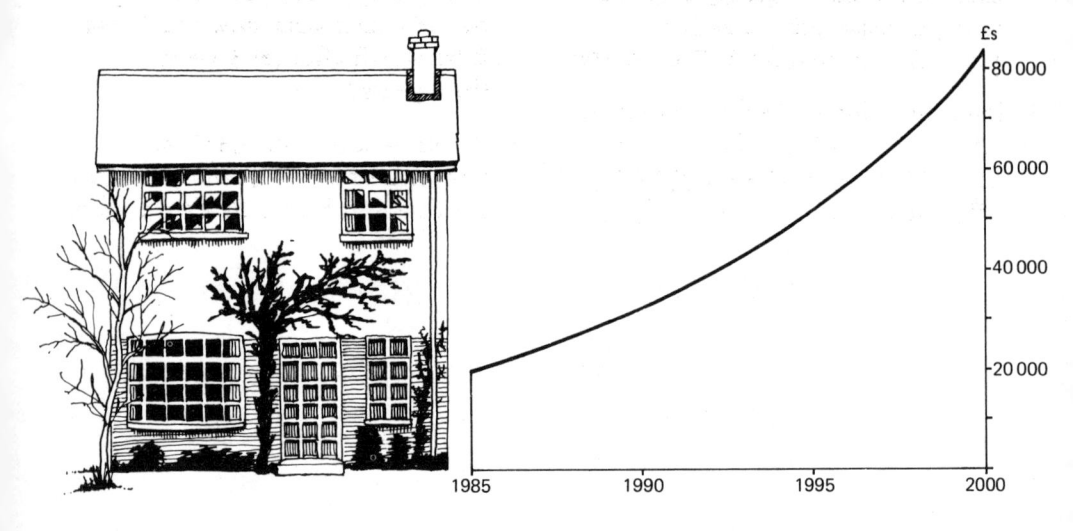

2. Sally buys a house for £24 000 which increases in value by 10% each year. Find its value (a) after 2 years, (b) after 4 years.

3. Cecil buys a house for £30 000 which increases in value by 8% each year. Find its value (a) after 2 years, (b) after 4 years.

4. Sonia buys a flat for £35 000 which increases in value by 12% each year. What will it be worth in (a) two years' time, (b) five years' time?

5. George buys a stamp for £50 which increases in value by 20% each year. What will it be worth in 5 years' time? Give your answer correct to the nearest £10.

6. Celia bought a new motor car for £10 000 which depreciated by 20% each year. Find its value after 1, 2, 3 and 4 years.

   Purchase price = £10 000
   Value after 1 year
   = £10 000 × (1 − 0.20)
   = £10 000 × 0.80
   = £8000
   Value after 2 years
   = £8000 × 0.80
   = £6400
   Value after 3 years
   = £6400 × 0.80
   = £5120
   Value after 4 years
   = £5120 × 0.80
   = £4096

7. Find the value of a new car after each of the first 4 years of its life if its purchase price was £12 000 and it depreciated by 20% each year.

8. Find the value of Asif's motorcycle after 3 years if it was bought for £1200 and depreciated in value by 15% each year.

9. Hyman & Co buy a machine for £50 000. If it depreciates in value by 20% each year, how much will it be worth after (a) 3 years, (b) 4 years?

10. A refrigerator costs £350 but depreciates by 10% each year. How much will it be worth after 5 years?

44 STATISTICS

A. PICTOGRAPHS

1. Study the pictograph where ☺ represents 4 hours of sunshine.

    Daily number of hours of sunshine in August:

    London ☺ ☽
    Majorca ☺ ☺ ☽
    Hong Kong ☺ ☽
    Bangkok ☺ ◁

    (a) How many hours of sunshine does each place have in August?
    (b) Which place has the most sunshine?
    (c) Which place has the least sunshine?

2. Study the pictograph where ☺ represents 2 hours of sunshine.

    Daily number of hours of sunshine in July:

    San Francisco ☺ ☺ ☺ ☺ ☽
    Antigua ☺ ☺ ☺ ☽
    Rio de Janeiro ☺ ☺ ☺
    Nairobi ☺ ☺ ◁

    (a) How many hours of sunshine does each place have in July?
    (b) Which place has the least sunshine?
    (c) Which place has the most sunshine?

3. Study the pictograph which shows the flying time from London to several holiday areas.

    Barbados ━ ━ ▬
    Singapore ━ ━ ━
    Cairo ━ ▬
    Los Angeles ━ ━ ━ ━

    where ━ represents 4 hours.

144

(a) Which place is nearest in flying time?
(b) Which place is furthest away in flying time?
(c) Find the flying time to each place.

4. Study the pictograph which shows the age range of the staff in a large store.

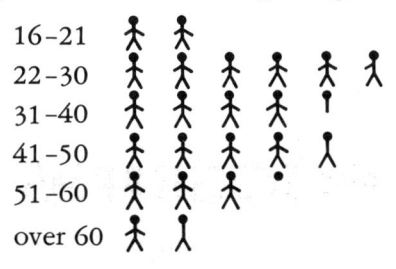

```
16-21    ẋ ẋ
22-30    ẋ ẋ ẋ ẋ ẋ ẋ
31-40    ẋ ẋ ẋ ẋ ẋ
41-50    ẋ ẋ ẋ ẋ ẋ
51-60    ẋ ẋ ẋ
over 60  ẋ ẋ
```
where ẋ represents 6 staff.

(a) Which age group contains the greatest number of staff?
(b) Which age group contains the least number of staff?
(c) How many staff are there in each age group?
(d) How many staff does the store employ?

5. The number of bottles of milk taken by a canteen during a certain week was:

Monday	24 pints
Tuesday	21 pints
Wednesday	26 pints
Thursday	24 pints
Friday	33 pints
Saturday	15 pints

Draw a pictograph to represent this information using 🍼 to represent 4 pints.

6. The number of cars passing my house in half an hour on a certain afternoon were:

British	30
European	35
Japanese	25
other	5

Draw a pictograph to represent this information using 🚗 to represent 10 cars.

B. PIE CHARTS

In questions 1–4, draw pie charts to illustrate the following information:

1. The ages of 30 girls in a youth club were: 13 years — 5, 14 years — 12, 15 years — 10, 16 years — 3.

2. The cars belonging to 24 families were: British 4, French 4, German 6, Italian 2, Japanese 6, other 2.

3. The bedtime drinks taken by 36 pupils were: coffee 18, tea 6, cold milk 9, other 3.
4. The favourite colours of 240 people were: red 50, blue 46, green 64, orange 20, yellow 30, other 30.
5. In the following pie chart measure the necessary angles to find the number of people with various kinds of pets if 10° represents one pet.

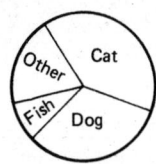

6. The pie chart that follows shows the type of accommodation used by 180 people. How many used each type?

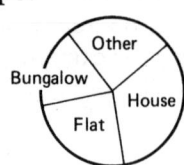

7. The pie chart that follows shows the shoe sizes of 30 pupils in a class.

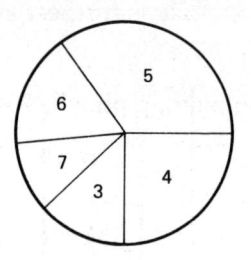

   (a) Which size was the most common?
   (b) Which size was the least common?
   (c) How many took a size 4?
   (d) How many took a size 3?

C. BAR CHARTS

1. The bar chart shows the rainfall at Koni during a particular week in June.

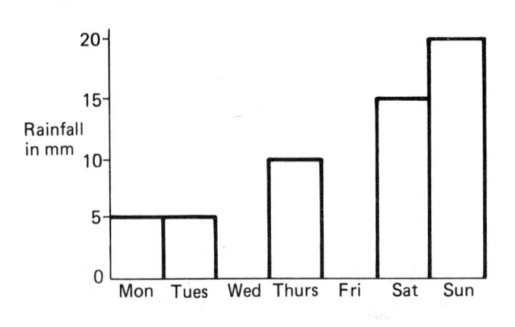

   (a) On how many days did it rain?
   (b) How much rain fell on each day?
   (c) What was the total rainfall for the week?

2. The bar chart shows the number of road users passing the school gates one morning.

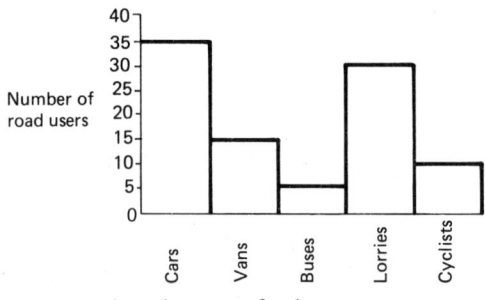

   Use the chart to find:
   (a) the number of cars passing
   (b) the number of cyclists passing
   (c) how many more lorries than vans passed
   (d) the total number of road users

3. The bar chart shows the flying time to various places from London.

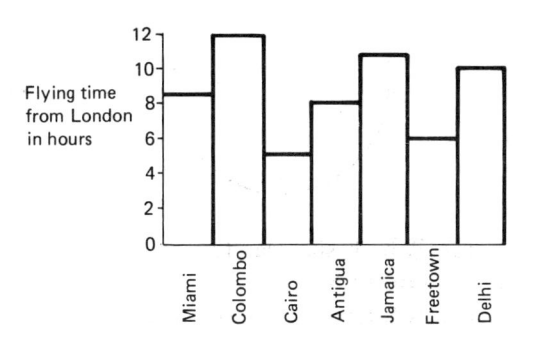

(a) Which place is the furthest in flying time from London?
(b) Which place is the nearest in flying time from London?
(c) What is the flying time from London to (i) Delhi, (ii) Cairo?

4. The bar chart shows the number of pupils in a form studying particular subjects.

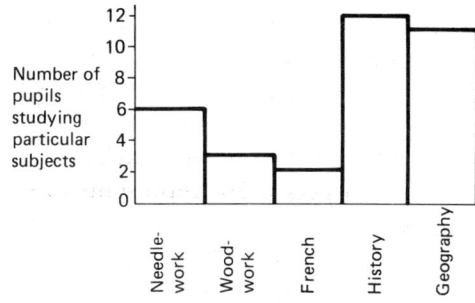

(a) How many study woodwork?
(b) How many study geography?
(c) What is the most popular subject and how many pupils study it?
(d) If every pupil studies *two* subjects, how many pupils are there in the form?

D. MEAN, MODE AND MEDIAN
MEAN

Mean

Find the arithmetic average or mean of the following sets of numbers:

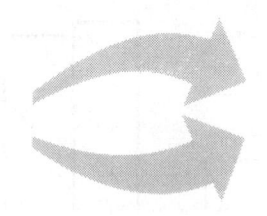

1. 4, 8, 10, 12, 16

$$\text{Mean} = \frac{4 + 8 + 10 + 12 + 16}{5}$$

$$= \frac{50}{5} = 10$$

2. 5, 10, 15, 20, 25
3. 8, 15, 7, 17, 9, 4
4. 23, 10, 12, 22, 16, 14, 13, 10
5. 21 m, 7 m, 25 m, 50 m, 9 m
6. 13 kg, 12 kg, 78 kg, 5 kg, 45 kg
7. 34p, 17p, 52p, 65p, 73p, 27p, 19p
8. 5.1 cm, 4.3 cm, 8.2 cm, 7.3 cm, 6.1 cm, 22.4 cm
9. 14.3 km, 62.8 km, 23 km, 32.6 km, 43.3 km
10. 8.3 g, 9.7 g, 5.4 g, 2.1 g, 7 g

Given below are the examination marks for five pupils in six subjects. Complete the table and use the average marks to place them in overall order of merit.

	Name	English	Maths	History	Geography	Science	Art	Total marks	Average marks
11.	Anne	54	73	52	46	64	77		
12.	Brian	62	87	64	60	56	43		
13.	Eira	37	56	47	82	62	46		
14.	Peter	86	62	73	53	36	38		
15.	John	51	57	54	59	63	70		

16. The heights, correct to the nearest cm, of 10 boys are: 154, 158, 156, 164, 160, 159, 172, 159, 155 and 173. What is (a) the sum of their heights, (b) their mean height?
17. The weights, correct to the nearest kg, of 8 girls are: 53, 48, 52, 56, 46, 60, 58 and 51. What is (a) the sum of their weights, (b) their mean weight?
18. My car travels 432 miles on 12 gallons of petrol. What is the average number of miles travelled on each gallon?
19. Susan's motorcycle travelled 168 km on 8 litres of petrol. On average, how many km is this per litre?
20. During the last week of May, Fred Sanson, who is a commercial traveller, recorded the following mileages: Sunday 24 miles, Monday 143 miles, Tuesday 84 miles, Wednesday 216 miles, Thursday 114 miles, Friday 60 miles, Saturday 73 miles. What was his average daily mileage?

In questions 21–25 find the mean length of the given lines:

21.

MODE

Mode

Find the mode of the following sets of numbers:

26. 2, 2, 3, 3, 3, 4, 4, 5
    The mode is the value that occurs most often
    i.e. mode is 3

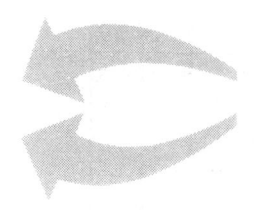

27. 4, 2, 3, 4, 3, 3, 4, 2, 4, 3, 4
28. 5.7, 5.5, 5.6, 5.7, 5.6, 5.6, 5.7, 5.8, 5.6
29. 32, 33, 34, 34, 37, 33, 32, 29, 26, 36, 33
30. 0.7, 0.6, 0.1, 0.4, 0.7, 0.6, 0.5, 0.7, 0.9, 0.6, 0.7

MEDIAN

Median

Find the median of the following sets of numbers:

31. 2, 2, 2, 3, 3, 3, 4, 5, 5

The median is the middle number of the 9 numbers when placed in numerical order, i.e. the median is 3.

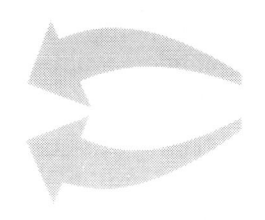

32. 9, 10, 11, 12, 83
33. 4.7, 8.2, 9.3, 10.4, 12.3, 15.6, 20
34. 8, 7, 4, 31, 2
35. 7.6, 23, 14.7, 9.3, 9.2, 8.3, 0.7

E. PROBABILITY

1. A bag contains twenty marbles. Twelve are red and the remainder green. If all the marbles are similar apart from colour, what is the probability of selecting (a) a red marble, (b) a green marble, (c) a blue marble?

    (a) Probability of selecting a red marble

    $$= \frac{\text{number of red marbles in bag}}{\text{total number of marbles in bag}} = \frac{12}{20} = \frac{3}{5}$$

    (b) Similarly, probability of a green marble

    $$= \frac{\text{number of green marbles in bag}}{\text{total number of marbles in bag}} = \frac{8}{20} = \frac{2}{5}$$

    (c) Probability of selecting a blue marble

    $$= \frac{\text{number of blue marbles in bag}}{\text{total number of marbles in bag}} = \frac{0}{20} = 0$$

2. There are 25 similar marbles in a bag. Ten are green, five are white and the remainder yellow. What is the probability of choosing (a) a white marble, (b) a yellow marble, (c) a red marble?

3. Eighteen of the thirty pupils in a class are girls. What is the probability that a pupil chosen at random is (a) a boy, (b) a girl?

4. A die is cast on the table. What is the probability of (a) a six, (b) an odd number, (c) a prime number?

5. An ordinary pack of 52 playing cards is cut. What is the probability of cutting (a) a red card, (b) a spade, (c) a five, (d) a Jack, Queen or King?

6. A bag contains 20 similar discs. 8 are red, 6 black, 1 white and the remainder blue. What is the probability that a disc drawn at random will be (a) black, (b) blue, (c) not red?

7. Thirty cars stand in a car park. 12 are Fords, 6 Vauxhalls, 8 British Leyland and the remainder Japanese. What is the probability that the first car to leave the park is (a) a Vauxhall, (b) a Ford, (c) not Japanese?

8. Peter is told by his friend Paul that his Metro has a puncture in one of its tyres. If all four are equally likely to have been punctured, what is the probability that the puncture is in (a) a front wheel, (B) a nearside wheel, (c) the rear offside wheel?

Part 2 REVISION PAPERS

REVISION PAPER 1

1. What is the value of the 4 in each of the following numbers?
   (a) 3472
   (b) 4265
   (c) 134
   (d) 14 275

2. (a) Give $\frac{18}{36}$ in its lowest terms.
   (b) Find $\frac{3}{4}+\frac{5}{4}$.

3. Express $3\frac{1}{6}$ as an improper fraction.

4. Find (a) 0.6 + 0.5, (b) 2.4 + 1.7.

5. Multiply 4.6 by (a) 10, (b) 100.

6. Convert $\frac{4}{5}$ into
   (a) a decimal,
   (b) a percentage.

7. Give 483 correct to
   (a) the nearest 10,
   (b) the nearest 100.

8. Find
   (a) $\begin{array}{r} p \\ 55 \\ 13\,+ \\ \hline \end{array}$

   (b) $\begin{array}{r} p \\ 55 \\ 13\,- \\ \hline \end{array}$

   (c) $\begin{array}{r} p \\ 22 \\ 3\,\times \\ \hline \end{array}$

9. Convert (a) 5 m into cm,
   (b) 7 km into m.

10. Find (a) 60% of 10 kg,
    (b) 25% of 64 cm.

Measuring a line (a) to the nearest 10 mm or, (b) to the nearest 100 mm

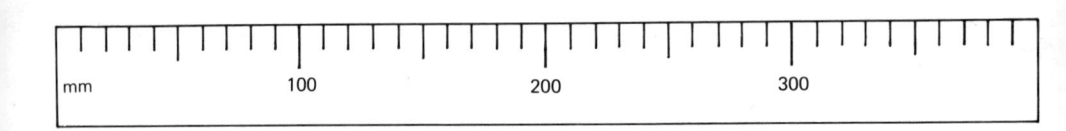

(a) Length to nearest 10 mm is 370 mm
(b) Length to nearest 100 mm is 400 mm

REVISION PAPER 2

1. Which fraction is the smaller:
   $\frac{7}{9}$ or $\frac{2}{3}$?

2. Find $\frac{3}{5} - \frac{1}{5}$.

3. Express $\frac{13}{4}$ as a mixed number.

4. Find (a) $2.3 + 5.4$, (b) $5.4 - 2.3$.

5. Multiply 37.2 by (a) 10, (b) 100.

6. Convert $\frac{9}{20}$ into
   (a) a decimal
   (b) a percentage.

7. Give 5280 correct to
   (a) the nearest 100,
   (b) the nearest 1000.

8. Find p
   (a) 84
       $23 +$
       $\overline{}$

   (b) 84
       $23 -$
       $\overline{}$

   (c) 21
       $4 \times$
       $\overline{}$

9. Convert (a) 15 cm into mm, (b) 44 m into cm.

10. Find (a) 50% of 3 t, (b) 75% of 32 m.

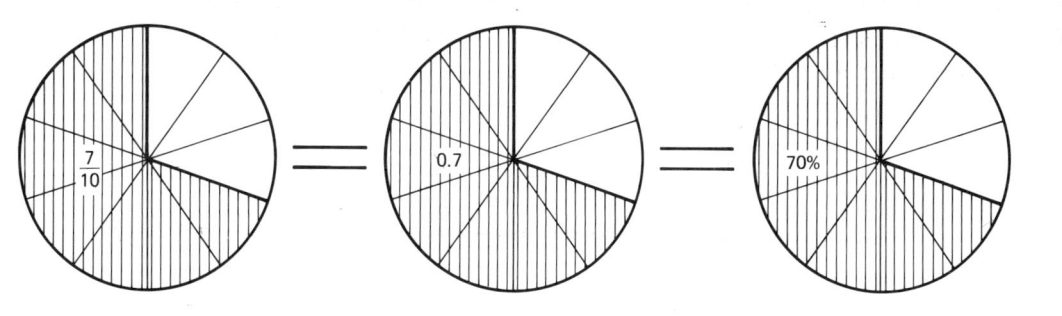

$\frac{7}{10}$ = 0.7 = 70%

155

REVISION PAPER 3

Solve the following cross number puzzle.

Across
5. 26×32
6. 7×7
7. $88 - 36$
9. The UK speed limit on motorways
10. The number of millimetres in one centimetre
11. $432 \div 6$
13. The freezing point of water in °F
15. A double century

Down
1. The fifth prime number
2. 17×17
3. $199 + 26$
4. $12 + 16$
6. $500 - 93$
8. The boiling point of water in °F
12. 22.2 cm in millimetres
13. The number of cm in 3 m
14. The number of players in a rugby union team
16. The number of 50p's in £10

REVISION PAPER 4

1. Find (a) $8.2 + 3.7$, (b) $8.7 - 3.2$.

2. Give $\dfrac{12}{30}$ in its lowest terms.

3. Find $\dfrac{5}{7} - \dfrac{2}{7}$.

4. Express $3\dfrac{1}{7}$ as an improper fraction.

5. Multiply 82.64 by (a) 10, (b) 100.

6. Convert $\dfrac{17}{20}$ into (a) a decimal, (b) a percentage.

7. Give 79.6 correct to
   (a) the nearest whole number,
   (b) the nearest 10.

8. Find

   (a) $\begin{array}{r} p \\ 37 \\ 54\ + \\ \hline \end{array}$

   (b) $\begin{array}{r} p \\ 54 \\ 37\ - \\ \hline \end{array}$

   (c) $\begin{array}{r} p \\ 44 \\ 5\ \times \\ \hline \end{array}$

9. Convert (a) 3.6 m into cm, (b) 5.4 km into m.

10. Find (a) 40% of 15 g,
    (b) 34% of 45 m.

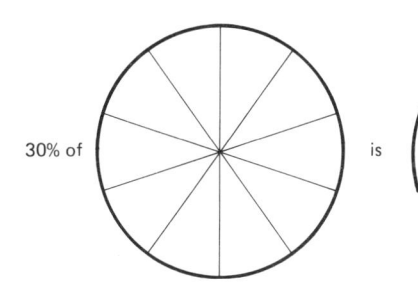

30% of ⬤ is ◔

REVISION PAPER 5

1. Which fraction is the larger, $\frac{5}{9}$ or $\frac{9}{13}$?

2. Find (a) $\frac{8}{13} + \frac{5}{13}$, (b) $\frac{8}{13} - \frac{5}{13}$.

3. Find (a) 5.2 + 7.8, (b) 7.2 − 5.8.

4. Divide 160 by (a) 10, (b) 100.

5. Convert $\frac{7}{10}$ into (a) a decimal, (b) a percentage.

6. Give 2874 correct to:
   (a) the nearest 10,
   (b) the nearest 1000.

7. Find
   (a) £
        1.25
        0.61
        3.13 +
        ─────

   (b) £
        0.84
        0.37 −
        ─────

   (c) £
        1.62
        4 ×
        ─────

8. Convert (a) 6.24 cm into mm, (b) 9.36 m into cm.

9. Find (a) 13 − 5, (b) 5 − 13, (c) −5 − 13.

10. Divide 84p between Sue and Bill in the ratio 3:4.

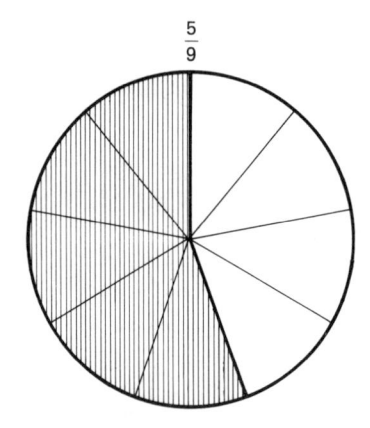

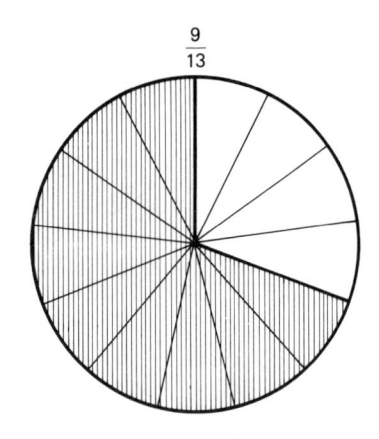

REVISION PAPER 6

1. Find $1 - \frac{3}{10}$.
2. Find (a) 0.8×2, (b) 0.4×8.
3. Divide 276 by (a) 10, (b) 100.
4. Convert $\frac{5}{8}$ into
   (a) a decimal,
   (b) a percentage.
5. Give 472 correct to:
   (a) the nearest 10,
   (b) two significant figures.
6. Find

   (a) £
   34.12
   16.44
   50.65 +
   ─────

   (b) £
   30.24
   18.92 −
   ─────

   (c) £
   3.74
   6 ×
   ─────

7. Convert (a) 0.45 km into m, (b) 0.6 cm into mm.
8. A record is bought for £4 and sold at a profit of 25%. Find the selling price.
9. The weights of the four puppies in a litter are 282 g, 260 g, 273 g and 317 g. What is the average weight of a puppy?
10. A coach travels 126 miles in 3 hours. Find its average speed. If it travels at the same speed for another $2\frac{1}{2}$ hours how far will it have travelled altogether?

REVISION PAPER 7

1. Find $\frac{8}{11} - \frac{5}{11}$.

2. Find $\frac{2}{3} \times \frac{9}{11}$, giving your answer in its lowest terms.

3. Find (a) 1.3 × 2, (b) 2.4 × 8.

4. Divide 1760 by (a) 10, (b) 100.

5. Convert 0.35 into (a) a percentage, (b) a common fraction in its lowest terms.

6. Give 4.264 93 correct to
   (a) one decimal place,
   (b) three significant figures.

7. Convert (a) 0.84 m into cm, (b) 0.465 km into m.

8. If I drive my car at a steady 45 mph how far will I travel in 3 hours? How long would it take me to drive 225 miles?

9. The diagram shows a cardboard box measuring 12 cm by 10 cm by 8 cm. Find:
   (a) the area of the end A,
   (b) the area of the side B,
   (c) the area of the top C,
   (d) the volume of the box.

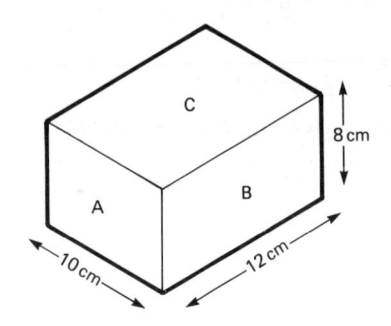

10. Express (a) 5 feet in inches, (b) 3 yards 1 foot in inches.

REVISION PAPER 8

1. What is the value of the 3 in (a) 1340, (b) 2530.

2. Find (a) 5.2×4, (b) 5.4×7.

3. Express 724 cm (a) in mm, (b) in m.

4. Find (a) $3\frac{1}{4} + 2\frac{1}{2}$, (b) $\frac{2}{3} \div \frac{5}{6}$.

5. Divide 1.26 by (a) 2, (b) 3.

6. Convert 0.85 into (a) a percentage, (b) a common fraction in its lowest terms.

7. Simplify (a) $6 - 10$, (b) $3 + (-4)$ (c) $-3 + (-4)$.

8. Give 17.777 47 correct to (a) two significant figures, (b) one decimal place.

9. Convert (a) 3 kg into g, (b) 5 t into kg.

10. Divide a 105 cm length of timber into two parts in the ratio 2:5. How much longer is the one part than the other?

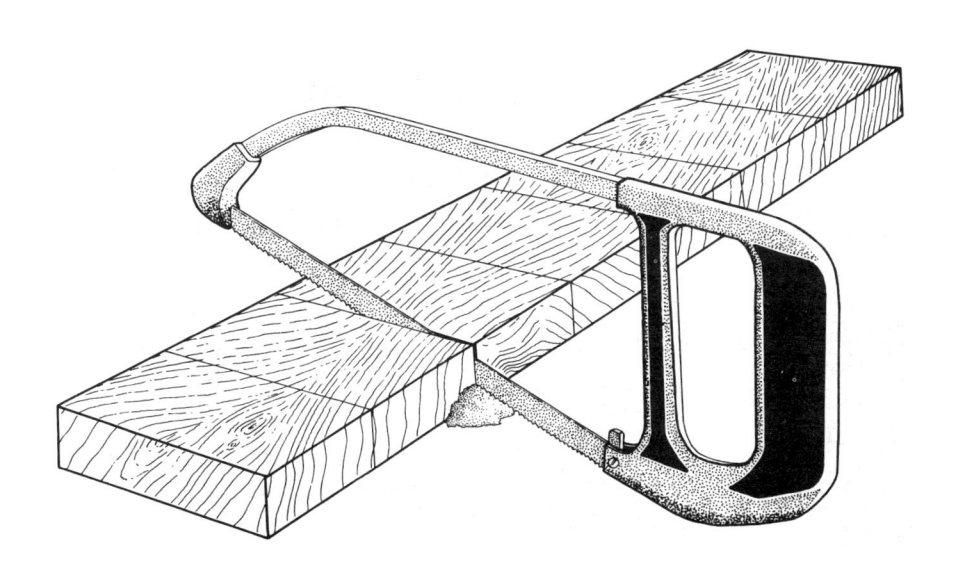

REVISION PAPER 9

Solve the following cross number puzzle.

Across
1. The number of days in June
2. 2 × 11
4. 48 + 18
5. 43 − 17
7. 500 − 33
8. The boiling point of water in °C
9. The number of aces in a pack of playing cards
10. How many centimetres are there in a metre?
12. Number of cm in an inch (to 2 decimal places)
15. Half a century
16. The sum of the first four prime numbers
17. Two score
18. Months in a year

Down
1. The number of days in a leap year
3. 880 ÷ 4
4. 4 × 4 × 4
6. 5 dozen
10. $\frac{3}{20}$ as a decimal
11. 0.0395 correct to one significant figure
13. 8 × 8 × 8
14. Two less than 7 squared

REVISION PAPER 10

1. Find the average of the numbers 10, 17, 34, 27, 37.
2. Find (a) 3.7×5, (b) 5.8×6.
3. Find $5\frac{3}{8} - 3\frac{1}{8}$.
4. Divide 8.4 by (a) 3, (b) 4.
5. Convert 65% into (a) a decimal, (b) a common fraction in its lowest terms.
6. Simplify (a) $6 - 12$, (b) $-6 - 12$, (c) $12 - 6$.
7. Give 843.9264 correct to
   (a) the nearest 10,
   (b) one decimal place.
8. Convert (a) 0.64 kg into g,
   (b) 0.264 t into kg.
9. If 1 inch = 2.54 cm, express
   (a) 14 inches in cm,
   (b) 100 cm in inches.
10. (a) Tom Cork earns £112 per week. How much is this in a year?
    (b) Fred Frizzell receives an annual salary of £17 004. How much is this each week?

REVISION PAPER 11

1. Write nineteen hundred and eighty-eight in figures.

2. A cube of sugar has a side of 2 cm. Find (a) its total surface area, (b) its volume.

3. Divide 48 by (a) 4, (b) 5.

4. Convert 96% into (a) a decimal, (b) a common fraction in its lowest terms.

5. The temperature early this morning was −6°C. It is now 10°C. How much has it risen?

6. Convert (a) 500 cm into m, (b) 7000 m into km.

7. Today is Friday 14 November. What was the date (a) last Friday, (b) a week last Wednesday? What will be the date (c) next Wednesday, (d) a week next Thursday?

8. In a form of 28 pupils the ratio of the number who study commerce to those who do not is 3:4. How many study commerce?

9. A car averages 14.4 km per litre of petrol. How far will it travel on (a) 10 litres, (b) 15 litres?

10. George's house has a rateable value of £180 and he pays £162 in rates. Find the rate in the £.

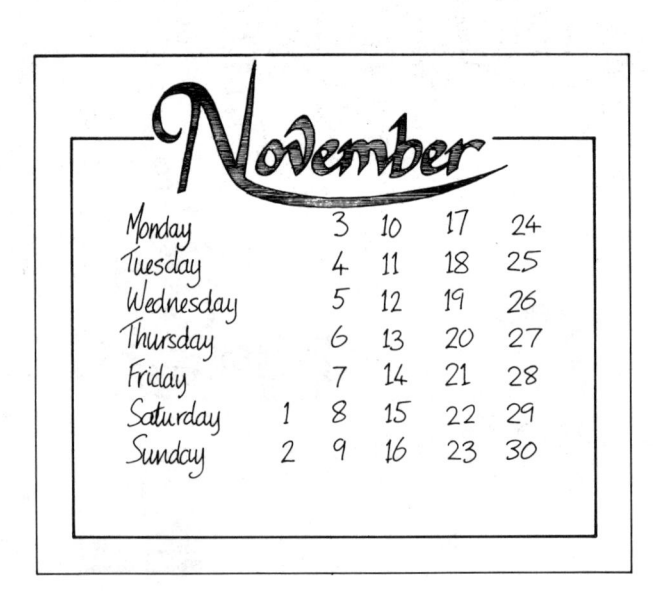

November

Monday		3	10	17	24
Tuesday		4	11	18	25
Wednesday		5	12	19	26
Thursday		6	13	20	27
Friday		7	14	21	28
Saturday	1	8	15	22	29
Sunday	2	9	16	23	30

REVISION PAPER 12

1. Share 63p between Anne and Tom in the ratio 5:4.

2. Express 72% as a decimal fraction.

3. Simplify (a) 0.28×7, (b) $0.28 \div 7$.

4. Express (a) 5000 cm^2 in m^2, (b) 3500 cubic centimetres in litres.

5. I am on the 11th floor of a block of flats. I go down 6 floors and then up nine floors. On which floor do I find myself?

6. Convert (a) 440 cm into m, (b) 764 m into km.

7. John Stonelake works 52 hours in a certain week. How much does he earn if he is paid £4.50 per hour?

8. A table lamp costs £48 plus value added tax at 20%. How much must I pay for it?

9. If £1 = \$1.5, convert (a) £342 into dollars, (b) \$300 into pounds.

10. Admission to a concert is £3.50 for adults and half price for children. A family of five consisting of father, mother and three children book tickets. How much change will there be from a £20 note?

REVISION PAPER 13

Solve the following cross number puzzle.

Across
1. The first three whole numbers
3. 10 − 4
4. The highest break in snooker
6. 30 − 6
8. 3^3
9. 121 ÷ 11
11. Twelve twelves
12. A score
13. The number of cm in an inch (to 2 decimal places)
15. 222 × 4
17. The third prime number
18. The value of the black in snooker
19. Usually the required score in a game of darts
21. The number of days in a leap year
23. The square of 9
24. 2 × 11 × 11
25. 5 × 3 × 5
27. 9 × 7 + 8
28. 3 × 7
30. $6\frac{1}{2}$ as a decimal correct to 2 decimal places
31. The smallest even whole number
32. 111 × 3

Down
1. 121 − 10
2. 8 × 4
4. 24 − 7
5. James Bond backwards!
7. $4\frac{1}{7}$ correct to 2 decimal places
8. 300 − 52
10. A dozen
12. 7 × 4
14. Half a thousand
16. 912 − 106
19. The first prime number after 30
20. The square of 11
21. 10 − 11.2 + 4.42
22. 443 − 376
23. 2538 ÷ 3
26. 5.227 correct to 3 sig. figs.
27. Three score years and ten
29. A baker's dozen

REVISION PAPER 14

1. Copy and complete the following bill:
   5 lb carrots at 30p per lb
   7 lb potatoes at 16p per lb
   1 cauliflower at 55p

2. Express (a) 630, (b) 0.63, in standard form

3. Add 500 g to 2 kg and give your answer (a) in grams, (b) in kilograms.

4. Which is the longer, 2 inches or 5 centimetres?

5. Find the simple interest on £600 invested for 3 years at 12% per year.

6. A TV set is rented at £2.73 per week or £9.42 per calendar month. How much is saved in one year if it is hired at the monthly rate rather than the weekly rate?

7. Peter travels 224 km in $3\frac{1}{2}$ hours. Find his average speed. How far would he expect to travel in $5\frac{1}{2}$ hours?

8. The time in Perth (Western Australia) is 8 hours ahead of London time.
   (a) If a test match in Perth starts at 11 am, what time is it in London?
   (b) If a test match at the Oval finishes at 6.30 pm, what time is it in Perth?

9. Find the mean, mode and median of the set of numbers 25, 65, 49, 31, 65.

10. A coach company charges passengers 6p per mile for a single journey and 5p per mile for a return journey. If it is 172 miles from Southampton to Stoke, find the cost of (a) the single fare, (b) the return fare.

REVISION PAPER 15

1. Divide £2.76 between Elaine and Clarrie in the ratio 5 : 7.
2. Take £19.32 from the sum of £13.78 and £7.54.
3. Find the simple interest on £400 borrowed for 3 years at 8% per year.
4. A train from Edinburgh to London due to arrive at 1652 is reported to be 26 minutes late. What is the new arrival time?
5. Find the area of a rectangle measuring 20 cm by 12 cm.
6. Find the volume of a cuboid measuring 20 cm by 15 cm by 10 cm.
7. If £1 ≡ 220 pesetas, convert (a) £34 into pesetas, (b) 9900 pta into pounds.
8. A motorcycle travels 26 km per litre of petrol. How far will it travel on (a) 5 litres, (b) 12 litres?
9. The total rateable value of the borough of Oakleigh is £7 643 000. Find the income from a penny rate.
10. The attendance at a pop concert was given as 12 000 correct to the nearest 1000. What was (a) the largest number, (b) the smallest number, that could have been there?

REVISION PAPER 16

1. Which number is the odd one out? 75, 125, 260, 300, 350

2. Which is longer (a) 1 yard or 1 metre, (b) 1 mile or 1 kilometre?

3. Add 50 cm to 5 m and give your answer (a) in centimetres, (b) in metres.

4. A cuboid measures 6 cm by 5 cm by 4 cm. Make a full size drawing of it. Find (a) its total surface area, (b) its volume.

5. Find the compound interest on £200 invested for 2 years at 15% per year.

6. In the local camera shop a deposit of 30% is required for any article bought on hire purchase. Find the deposit on a camera costing £120.

7. Moscow time is 2 hours ahead of Paris time. What time is it (a) in Paris when it is 4 am in Moscow, (b) in Moscow when it is 4 pm in Paris?

8. Today is Tuesday 4 May. What date will it be (a) next Saturday, (b) a week next Thursday? What was the date (c) last Tuesday, (d) a week last Friday?

9. From a factory worker's weekly wage of £91.40 there are deductions of £12.86. Find his 'take home' pay.

10. In a school there is 1 teacher for every 18 pupils. If there are 936 pupils, how many teachers are there?

NAME	P. J. Brookes		CLOCK NUMBER	2143
NATIONAL INSURANCE NUMBER	NA 6081 14 D		TAX CODE	ALD 24351Z
HOURLY RATE	£2—40	HOURS PER WEEK	38	NATIONAL INSURANCE THIS WEEK	£5—32
TOTAL NATIONAL INSURANCE P/W	£10—64		TOTAL N.I. CONTRIBUTIONS	£159—60
O.T. RATE	£3—61	O.T. THIS WEEK	—	GROSS PAY	£91—20
TOTAL WAGES RECEIVED	£1371—09	TOTAL TAX THIS WEEK	£7—54	TOTAL TAX PAID	£113—10
TOTAL DEDUCTIONS	£12—86		NET PAY	£78—34

REVISION PAPER 17

1. Express (a) 5740, (b) 23.6, in standard form.

2. Subtract 12 mm from 12 cm and give your answer (a) in millimetres, (b) in centimetres.

3. Multiply the sum of 4.63 and 5.37 by their difference.

4. Find (a) $2\frac{1}{3} + 1\frac{1}{2}$ (b) $2\frac{1}{2} - 1\frac{1}{3}$ (c) $\frac{1}{3} \div 3$ (d) $\frac{4}{5} \times \frac{7}{12}$

5. Increase £5.25 by 20%.

6. Divide 384 apples between the Black family and the White family in the ratio 7:9.

7. Tom spends £704 on petrol in a year. If petrol costs £2.20 a gallon, how many gallons does he buy? If he travels 43 miles on each gallon find his mileage for the year.

8. If £1 ≡ 2.5 Deutschmarks, convert (a) £124 into Deutschmarks, (b) 180 DM into pounds.

9. What is the probability of drawing (a) a seven, (b) a Jack, Queen or King that is red, from an ordinary pack of 52 playing cards?

10. A car travels at 90 km per hour. How far will it travel between (a) 1200 and 1400, (b) between 1430 and 1700?

REVISION PAPER 18

1. Reduce each of these fractions to their lowest terms:

   $\dfrac{9}{18}, \dfrac{16}{20}, \dfrac{20}{25}, \dfrac{60}{84}$.

2. Change (a) 5.2 cm into mm, (b) 154 mm into cm, (c) 0.46 m into cm.

3. Find (a) $5.3 + 1.9$
   (b) $8.2 - 2.6$
   (c) 12.7×3
   (d) $7.65 \div 3$

4. Find (a) the perimeter, (b) the area, of a rectangle measuring 10 cm by 8 cm.

5. A coach from Manchester to Victoria due to arrive at 1444 is reported to be 35 minutes late. What is the actual time of arrival?

6. The deposit for a washing machine bought on hire purchase is £36. In addition 24 monthly repayments of £8.63 are required. How much does the machine actually cost?

7. Today is Saturday. Last Tuesday the date was 14 October. What date will it be (a) next Saturday, (b) a week next Tuesday? What date was it (c) last Monday, (d) a week last Wednesday?

8. My friend bought a house for £40 000. If it increases in value by 10% each year, how much will it be worth (a) in a year, (b) in two years' time, (c) in three years' time?

9. A ship travels at a steady 20 nautical miles per hour. How many days will it take for a journey of 8640 nautical miles?

10. Find the cash price of a dishwashing machine marked at £240 plus value added tax at 15%.

REVISION PAPER 19

1. (a) Add 100 to each of the numbers: 1340, 724, 93.
   (b) Subtract 1000 from each of the numbers: 5730, 1043, 27 340.

2. Find (a) $8.4 + 4.7$ (b) $8.4 - 4.7$
   (c) 1.4×5 (d) $37 \div 10$
   (e) $2.4 \div 3$

3. Express 32.725
   (a) correct to the nearest whole number,
   (b) correct to 3 significant figures,
   (c) correct to 2 decimal places.

4. Find the compound interest on £400 invested for 2 years at 12% per year.

5. A car travels 15 km per litre of petrol. How many litres are required for a journey of 330 km? How much will this cost at 50p per litre?

6. The rateable value of my house is £160. How much will I pay in rates when the rate in the £ is 70p?

7. I expect to get 40 000 miles out of a set of tyres on my car. If each tyre costs £35, how much per mile, in pence, do I spend on tyres?

8. Peter Smith must pay income tax at 30p in the £ on £80 of his income each week. How much tax does he pay?

9. The gross insurance premium for my car is £355. What is the net premium if a discount of 60% is allowed?

10. A newsagent pays his delivery boys 2p for each newspaper delivered. One boy leaves the shop with 115 newspapers and returns with 7. How much does he earn?

REVISION PAPER 20

1. (a) Express 2 m as a percentage of 5 m.
   (b) Find 40% of £25.50.
2. What percentage of 1 litre is 300 cm^3?
3. Add 7.2 to 8.9 and subtract the result from 20.
4. Give the following am/pm times as they would appear on a 24-hour clock:
   (a) 7.35 am   (b) 3.15 pm
   (c) 9.50 pm   (d) 12 midnight
5. Express $\frac{7}{20}$ (a) as a percentage, (b) as a decimal.
6. A retailer buys a skirt for £20 and sells it at a loss of 30%. Find the selling price.
7. The cash price of a caravan is £2400. If bought on hire purchase the terms are:
   Deposit 20% plus 36 monthly repayments of £74.40.
   How much does the caravan actually cost?
8. If £1 ≡ 11 f, convert (a) £120 into francs, (b) 803 f into pounds.
9. My car depreciated in value by 20% each year. If it cost £10 000 when new, how much was it worth (a) after 1 year, (b) after 2 years?
10. A concrete block measures 24 cm by 18 cm by 4 cm. Find (a) its total surface area, (b) its volume in cm^3.

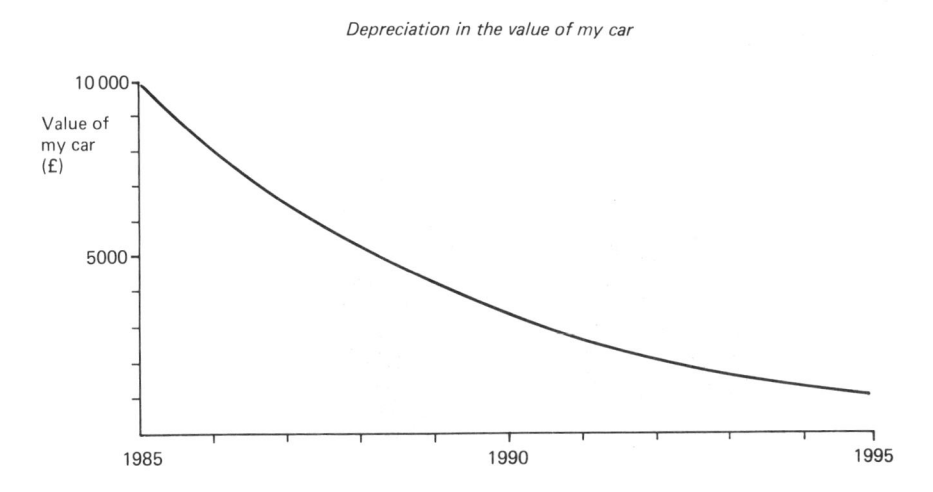

Depreciation in the value of my car